ENGLISH HOMEWORK

ANNE ZEMAN

KATE KELLY

AN IRVING PLACE PRESS BOOK

SCHOLASTIC INC.
NEW YORK TORONTO LONDON AUCKLAND
SYDNEY MEXICO CITY NEW DELHI HONG KONG

ISBN 978-0-545-37474-3

12 11 10 9 8 7 6 5 4 3 2 1 11 12 13 14 15 16/0

Printed in the U.S.A. 08

This edition first printing, September 2011

Cover design, Red Herring Design; Cover illustration, Sarajo Frieden
Interior design, Bennett Gewirtz, Gewirtz Graphics, Inc.; Interior illustration, Greg Paprocki

Contents

Part 4. Parts of Speech

Part 5. Writing Tools

Part 6. Creative Writing

Part 7. Practical Writing

Part 8. Reading

Introduction

It's homework time—but you have questions. You need some help, but no adults are around, and you can't reach your classmates on the phone. Where can you go for help?

What Questions Does This Book Answer?

In *Everything You Need to Know About English Homework*, you will find a wealth of information, including the answers to some of the most commonly asked English homework questions.

- What are homonyms, homophones, and antonyms? Homonyms, homophones, and homographs are defined on page 27. A table of homonyms appears on pages 28–30. Antonyms are the subject of page 36.
- How do you use a dictionary to find the meaning of a word? A guide to using a dictionary is found on pages 34–38.
- How do you write a book report? A feature on book reports is found on page 108.
- How do you find the main idea? The main idea of a paragraph is defined and illustrated on pages 66–67.
- When and how do you use quotation marks? The proper use of quotation marks and other common punctuation marks is listed on pages 60–64.
- How do you spell *exaggerate* and other difficult words? Commonly misspelled words are the subject of a table on page 27.
- How do you write a poem? Guidelines for writing poems are found on page 91.
- Where do you put an apostrophe to show possession? Find out how apostrophes are used to show possession on page 60.
- What is the difference between a simile and a metaphor? Metaphor and simile are defined on pages 80 and 82.
- How do you form contractions? Contractions are defined and illustrated on page 33.

What Is the *Everything You Need to Know About...Homework* series?

The *Everything You Need to Know About...Homework* series is a set of unique reference resources written especially to answer the homework questions of fourth-, fifth-, and sixth-graders. The series provides ready information to answer commonly asked homework questions in a variety of subjects. Here you'll find facts, charts, definitions, and explanations, complete with examples and illustrations that will supplement schoolwork colorfully, clearly, and comprehensively.

A Note to Parents

It's important to support your children's efforts to do homework. Welcome their questions and see that they are equipped with a well-lighted desk or table, pencils, paper, and any other books or equipment that they need—such as rulers, calculators, reference books or textbooks, and so on. You might also set aside a special time each day for doing homework, a time when you're available to answer questions that may arise. But don't do your children's homework for them. Remember, homework should create a bond between school and home. It is meant to enhance the lessons taught at school on a daily basis, and to promote good work and study habits. Although it is gratifying to have your children present flawless homework papers, the flawlessness should be a result of your children's explorations and efforts—not your own.

The *Everything You Need to Know About...Homework* series is designed to help your children complete their homework on their own to the best of their abilities. If they're stuck, you can use these books with them to help find answers to troubling homework problems. And remember, when the work is done, praise your children for a job well done.

ENGLISH HOMEWORK

Languages and Alphabets

Chapter 1 Languages

LANGUAGES SPOKEN AROUND THE WORLD

About 4,000 languages are spoken throughout the world today. Many of them are spoken by only a few people and within a small area.

Some people speak more than one language. In the United States, for example, many families come from other countries. Although these families learn English when they settle here, they may still speak the language of their home country. In some countries, people speak one language at home and another for business and politics. All people who can speak two languages are ***bilingual***.

Today, English is often spoken in international business and politics. It is called an ***international language***. For example, if a Japanese person wants to buy land from a person in Poland, unless they have an interpreter, the Japanese person and the Polish person will probably speak to each other in English. Spanish and French are two other international languages.

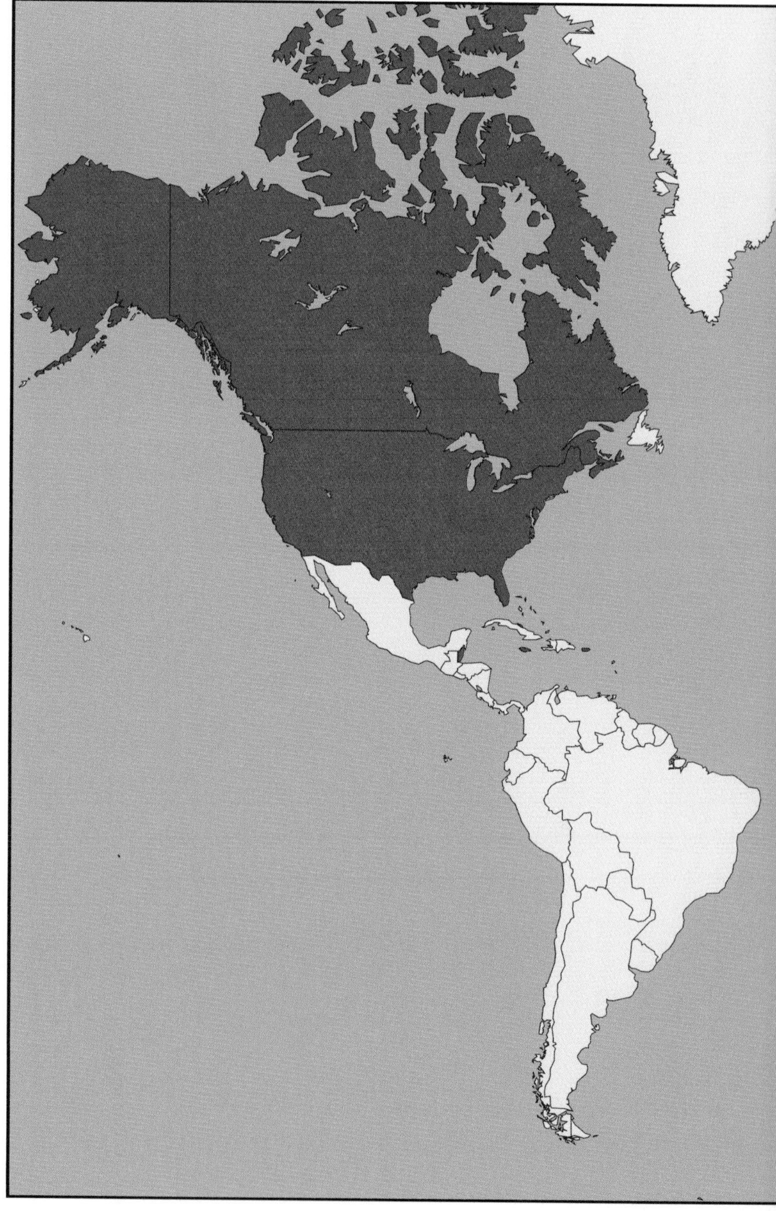

Places around the world where English is spoken are in red.

The World's Most Commonly Spoken Languages

Language	Number of Speakers
Mandarin	more than 1,000,000,000
English	490,000,000
Hindi	nearly 435,000,000
Spanish	nearly 400,000,000
Russian	285,000,000
Arabic	230,000,000

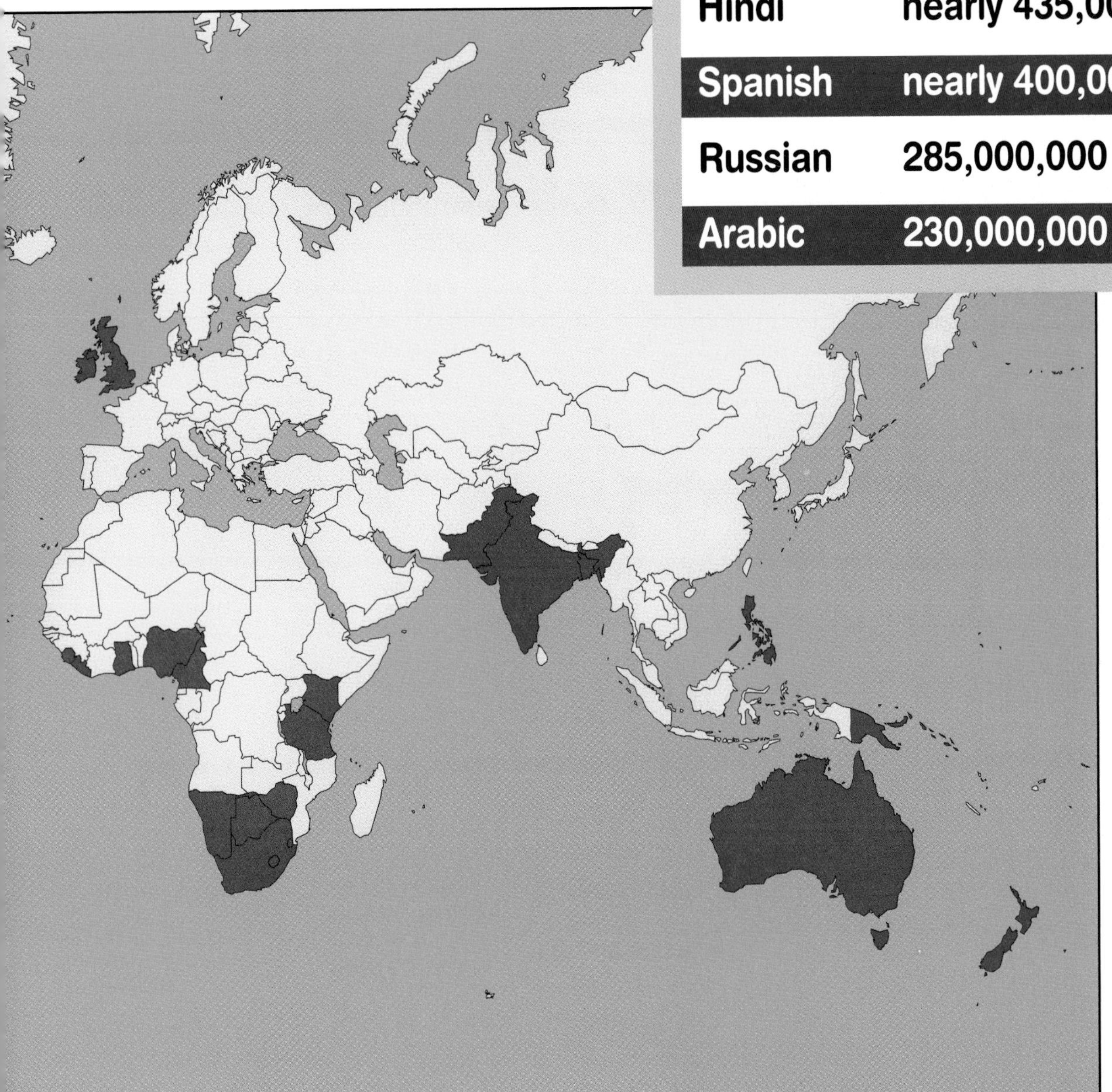

Indo-European Languages

The languages of the world are grouped into ***families***. These families include languages that are related to each other. Most ***linguists*** (see p. 5) believe that the languages in each family grew out of one ancient language.

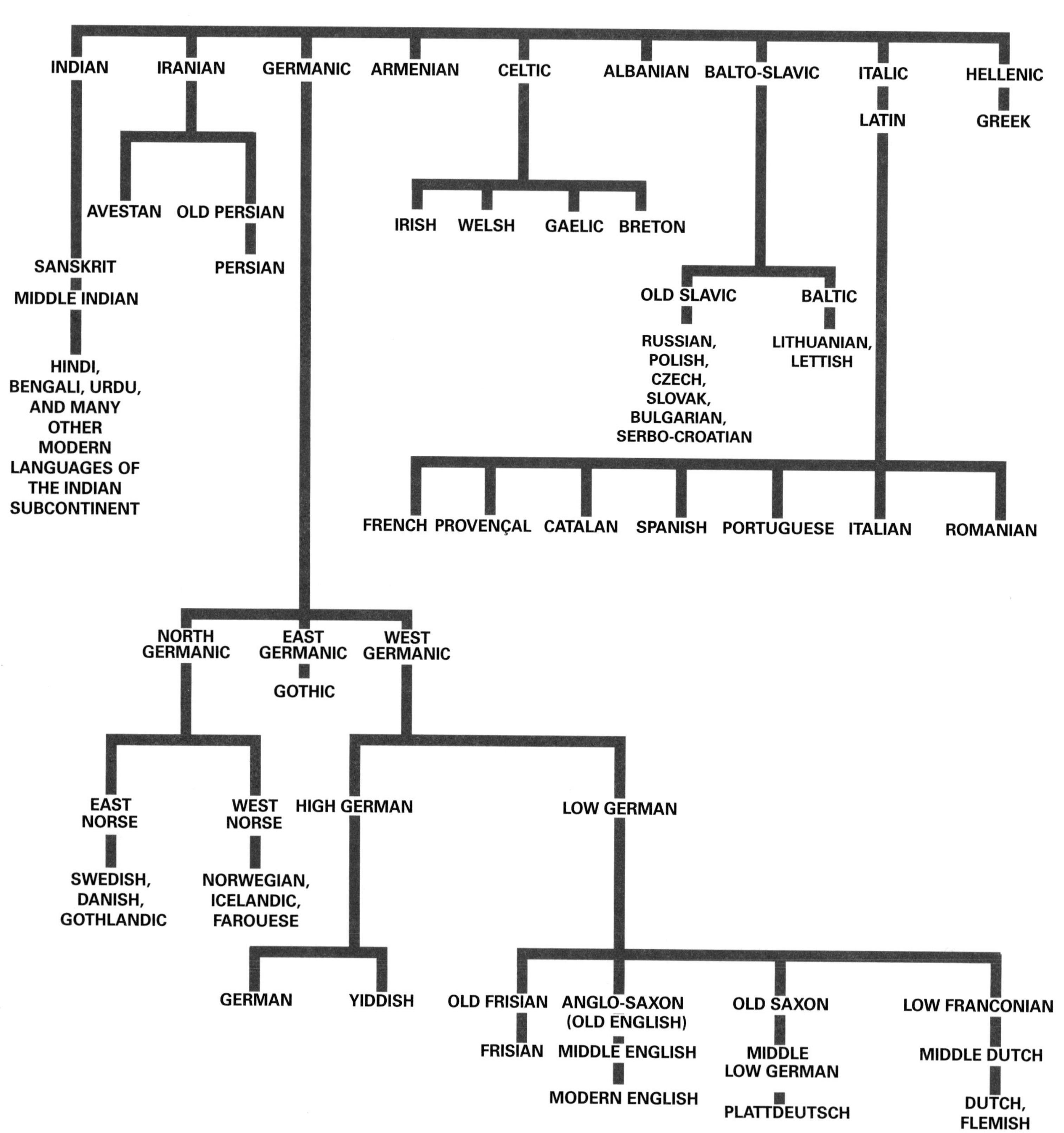

Here is the word ***mother*** in some Indo-European languages. Can you see how they are related?

Dutch	**moeder**
French	**mère**
German	**mutter**
Hindi	**mata**
Italian	**madre**
Spanish	**madre**

Some words are related through ancestral descent, derivation, or borrowing. These words are called *cognates*.

The Scientists of Language

The study of language is called ***linguistics***. The people who study language are called linguists. The different types of linguists include the following:

Grammarians. People who study grammar. ***Grammar*** means the parts of a language and the rules for speaking and writing that language.

Phoneticians or ***phonetists***. Those who study ***phonetics***. Phonetics is the study of sounds in speech. Phoneticians study how the tongue, lips, and teeth are positioned in order to make different sounds. The study of speech sounds, ***phonemics***, is part of phonetics. When you study ***phonics*** in school, you are studying an area of phonetics.

Semanticians. Linguists who study ***semantics***. Semantics is the study of the meanings of sounds and words. ***Morphemics***, the study of units of sound that carry meaning, is part of semantics.

Morphologists. People who study ***morphology***. Morphology is the study of how language changes over time and in different places. For example, some morphologists are concerned with the difference between Old English (used about 450–1100), Middle English (used about 1100–1500), and Modern English (used today). Other morphologists are concerned with the different ways the same language is spoken in different places. For example, they might compare English in such countries as the United States, Canada, Great Britain, and Australia, or Spanish in Spain, Mexico, and Peru.

Philologists. Those who study ***philology***. Philology is the study of how the language of a culture affects its literature.

Chapter 2 **Alphabets**

A History of Our Alphabet

In English, we use a set of 26 letters to spell words:

A B C D E F G H I J K L M N O P Q R S T U V W X Y Z

This set of letters is our ***alphabet***.

Our alphabet is called the Latin or Roman alphabet. Except for the letters ***j***, ***u***, and ***w***, it was the alphabet used by the Romans 2,000 years ago. At first, the Roman alphabet had only 21 letters. Around 100 B.C., the letters ***y*** and ***z*** were added. ***J***, ***u***, and ***w*** were added much later to represent sounds spelled before with ***y*** and ***v***, as well as to represent new sounds.

WHERE DID THE ROMAN ALPHABET COME FROM?

The Romans used the Etruscan alphabet to design their own alphabet. The Etruscans were people who lived in northern Italy about 8,000 years ago. The Etruscan alphabet grew out of the ancient Greek alphabet.
The ancient Greeks borrowed the alphabet of an even more ancient group of people, the Phoenicians. About 10,000 years ago, the Phoenicians lived in Byblos, a city in modern Lebanon. Byblos was a center for trading ***papyrus***, a reed that was made into paperlike sheets of material. Our word ***paper*** comes from the word papyrus. The Greek word for book, ***byblos***, comes from the name of the city Byblos. ***Byblos*** is also the root of our word ***Bible***.

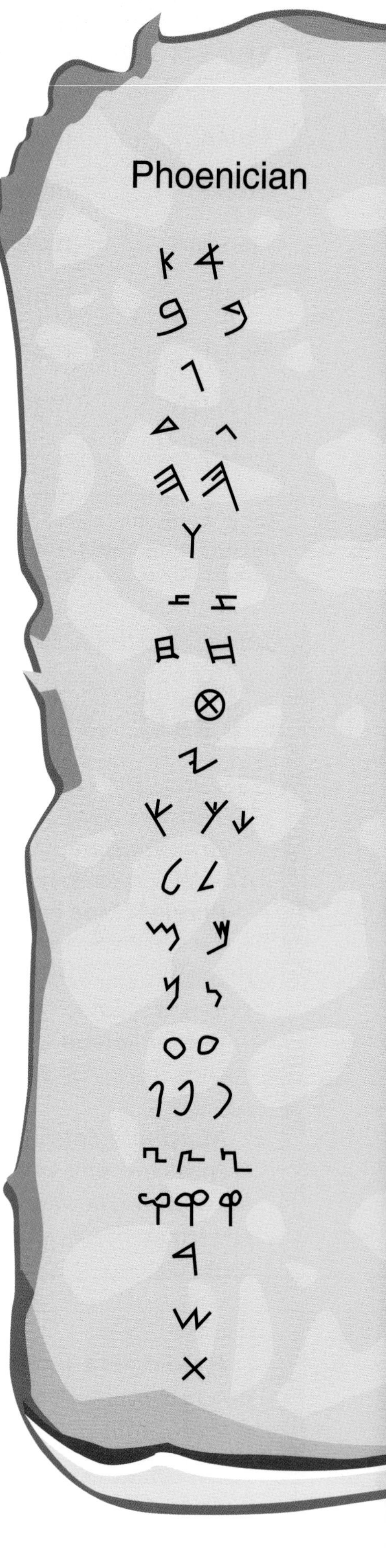

Early Greek	Later Greek	Roman	English
A	A	A	A
Ƨ ᗺ	B	B	B
ꓶ	Γ	CG	CG
Δ	Δ	D	D
ᴲ	E	E	E
ꟻ	Ϝ	FV	F,U,V, W,Y
I	I		Z
⊟	⊟	H	H
⊗	⊗		(Th)
ϟ	ϟ	I	I,J
ꓘ	K	K	K
✓ ⊣ ⌉	L Λ	L	L
ᴍ	M	M	M
И	N	N	N
O	O	O	O
ꟼ	Γ	P	P
M	M		(S)
Ϙ	Ϙ	Q	Q
◁	▷	R	R
Σ	Σ	S	S
T	T	T	T

HIEROGLYPHICS, PICTOGRAPHS, AND SYLLABARIES

Hieroglyphics are sets of special picture symbols used to write down stories or information. Among the best-known hieroglyphics are those used by the ancient Egyptians, who created an elaborate set of picture symbols to describe daily life, farming, and the wealth of pharaohs. Egyptian hieroglyphics are easy to recognize but they are difficult to read. Reading hieroglyphics is so difficult, in fact, that the word ***hieroglyphics*** also means any handwriting, figures, codes, or characters that are hard to understand or decipher.

Pictographs are picture signs and symbols that tell a story, although the signs and symbols aren't organized into a set. The pictures drawn on cave walls by early humans are pictographs telling stories of daily life, hunting, fishing, gathering, and so on. Pictographs are still used today to chart information by using picture symbols to represent special kinds of information.

Syllabaries are sets of symbols. In a syllabary, each symbol represents a specific syllable that can be used in many different words. A syllabary was used instead of an alphabet in the writing systems of some ancient cultures and is still used today. The two sets of characters used in writing Japanese are modern examples of syllabaries.

The early cuneiform symbol for an ox evolved from pictographs.

CAPITAL AND SMALL LETTERS

Until about 200 years ago, only a small group of people could read and write. Some of these people, called ***engravers***, cut (engraved) words and dates into stone tablets or into the faces of buildings or monuments. The engravers used capital letters, which they carved in simple lines and curves into the stone.

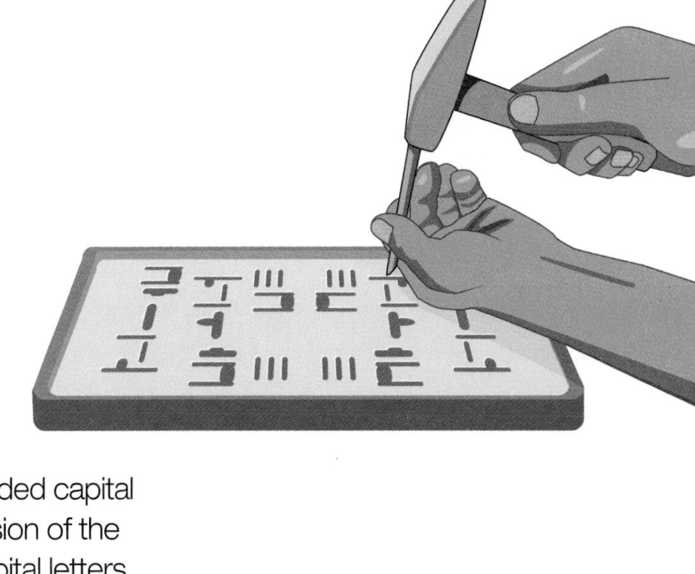

Later, people called ***scribes*** were trained to write on papyrus and parchment. Papyrus and parchment were very expensive, so scribes had to fit as many words as they could on each precious page. Scribes also had to copy huge books such as the Bible, so they needed to write quickly.

Although capital letters were easy to engrave in stone, they were too large and difficult to form quickly when written with quill pens. So scribes developed ***cursive*** letters that flowed more easily together. At first, they rounded capital letters into ***uncials***. By 1000 A.D., they had created a version of the Roman alphabet in small letters. By combining cursive capital letters with small letters, scribes had a system of writing that saved space and time.

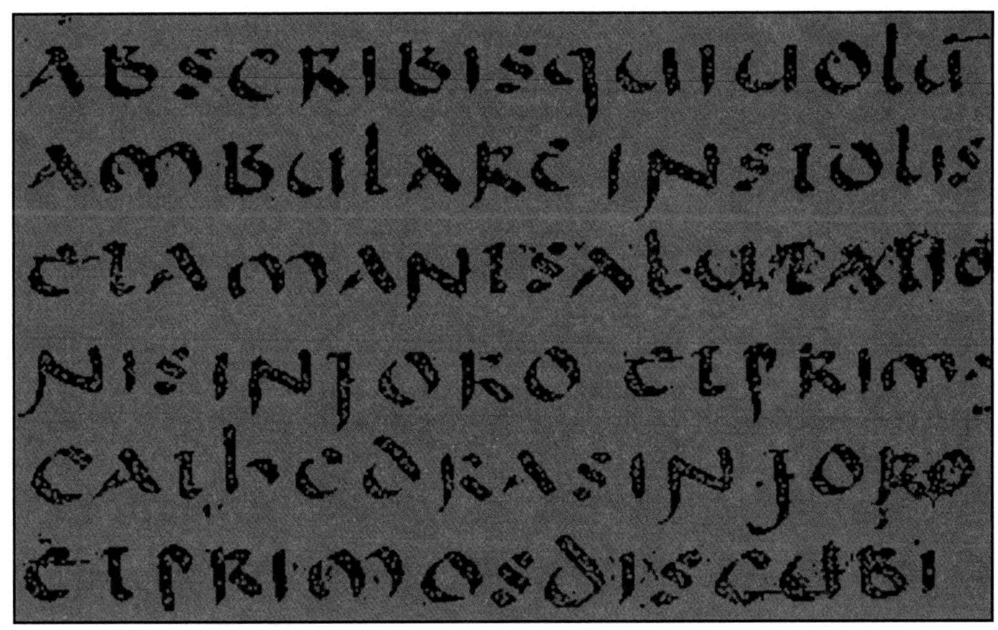

An early scribe wrote uncials on this sample of a manuscript created with ink on parchment.

UPPERCASE AND LOWERCASE

Today we call capital letters ***uppercase*** letters. We call small letters ***lowercase*** letters. The terms ***uppercase*** and ***lowercase*** came about with the invention of printing presses.

Alphabet Spin-offs

Many alphabets are used in the world today. Some are closely related to the Roman alphabet. For example, the ***Celtic alphabet*** is still used in Ireland and Scotland to write the Gaelic language. The ***Cyrillic alphabet*** — used in Serbia, Bulgaria, the Ukraine, and Russia — was adapted from the Greek alphabet. The ***Chinese*** created an alphabet based on pictures called ***characters***. The ***Japanese*** and ***Korean alphabets*** are based on characters, too.

READING FROM RIGHT TO LEFT AND TOP TO BOTTOM

Roman, ***Greek***, and related alphabets are read from left to right. So is the ***Hindi*** alphabet, which is used in parts of India and Africa. But some alphabets, such as ***Arabic*** and ***Hebrew***, are read from right to left. Still other alphabets, like the ***Chinese***, are read from top to bottom.

הפך בה והפך
בה דכולא בה
כתבו לכמ את
השירה הזאת

Hebrew is read from right to left.

Chinese is read from top to bottom.

Sign and Symbol Languages

Sign Language

When people have difficulty hearing or cannot hear at all, spoken language is often not effective. ***Sign language*** was developed as another way for the hearing impaired to communicate. Signs that stand for letters and whole words are made by shaping fingers and hands in different ways. People can have a conversation using sign language.

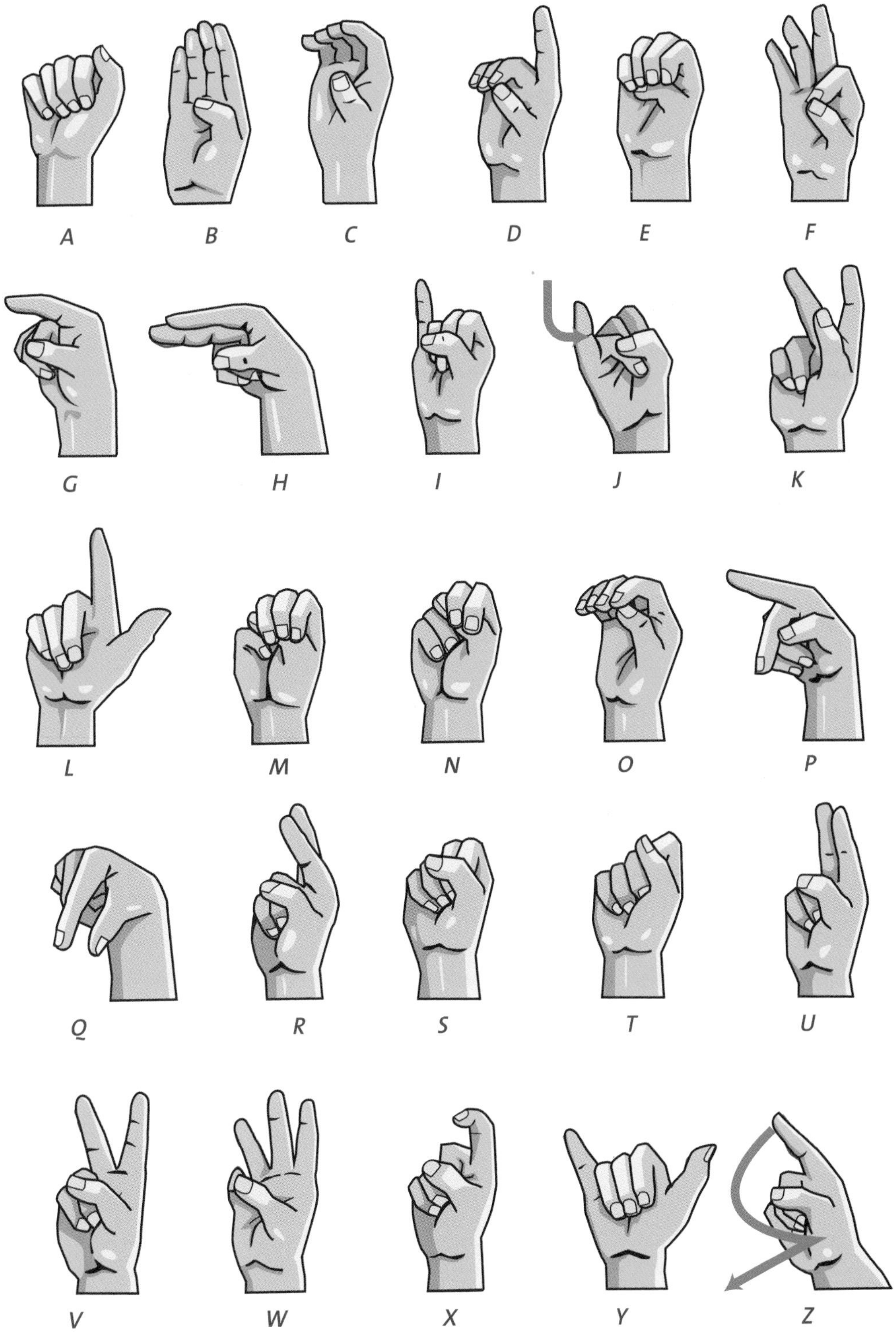

A *B* *C* *D* *E* *F*

G *H* *I* *J* *K*

L *M* *N* *O* *P*

Q *R* *S* *T* *U*

V *W* *X* *Y* *Z*

Braille

Reading words on a page can be difficult for people with poor eyesight and impossible for people who are blind. In the late 1820s, ***Louis Braille***, himself a blind man, invented a special alphabet for people with sight problems. The ***Braille alphabet*** consists of raised dots that are read by touch, not sight. Each letter has its own set of dots. The letters are written on paper held by a frame. The writer uses a pointed stick, or ***stylus***, to make the dots. Today many blind people use machines similar to typewriters to make the dots.

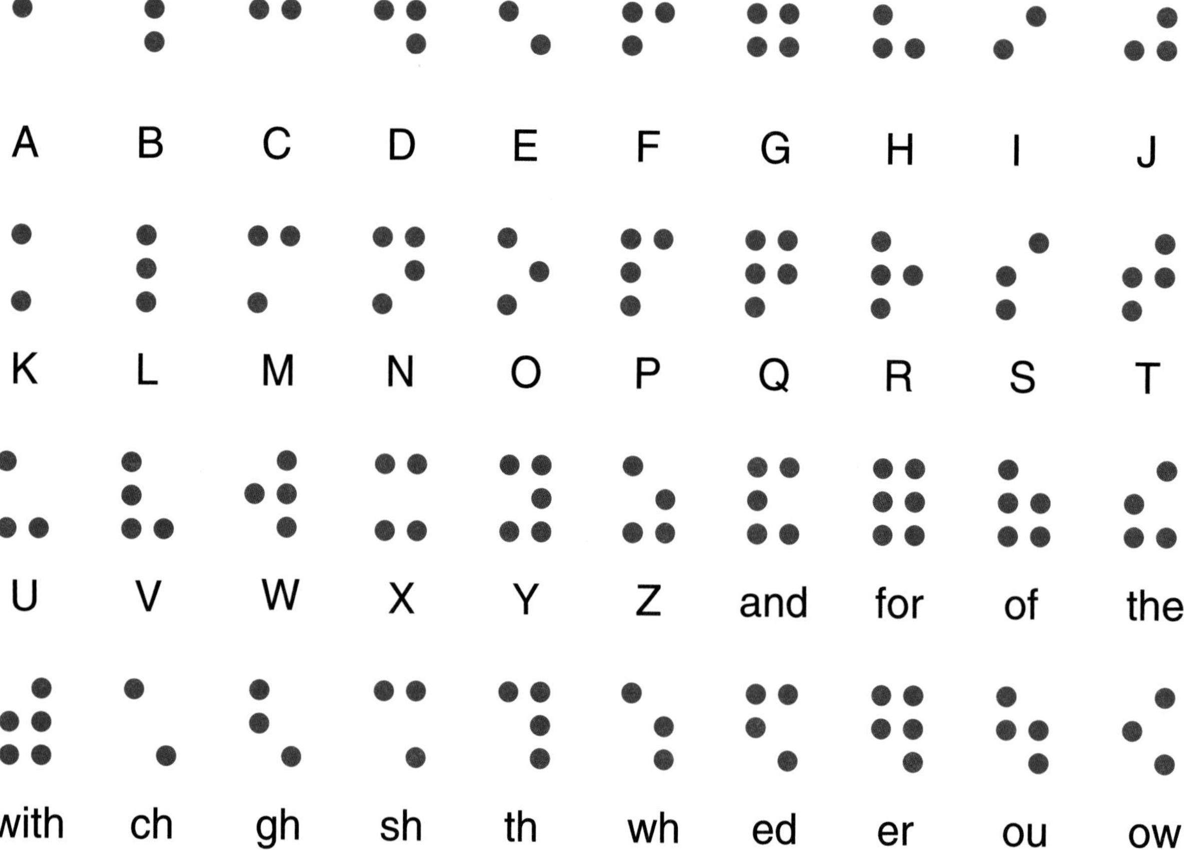

Native American Sign Language and Smoke Signals

Ancient Native American cultures, including the Maya and Aztecs of Mexico and Central America, created writing systems made up of ***glyphs***, or pictures. In North America, Sequoya, a Cherokee, invented a writing system made up of 86 signs that stood for the different sounds in the Cherokee language. Each tribe spoke a different language, so Native Americans from different tribes invented a simple sign language to facilitate communication.

Native Americans on the Great Plains also communicated by smoke signals. The signals could be seen over many miles. By using smoke signals for basic communication, messengers were not needed to travel long distances over dangerous routes.

arrow *trade* *friend*

buffalo *horse* *tepee*

Native American *caucasian* *peace*

Semaphore

Sailors can't shout loudly enough over the noise of wind and waves to be heard on passing ships, and hand signs are impossible to read over the distances at sea. So sailors use ***semaphore***. In semaphore, sailors use brightly colored flags in different patterns and angles to represent different letters and messages. The flags can be seen easily across the water.

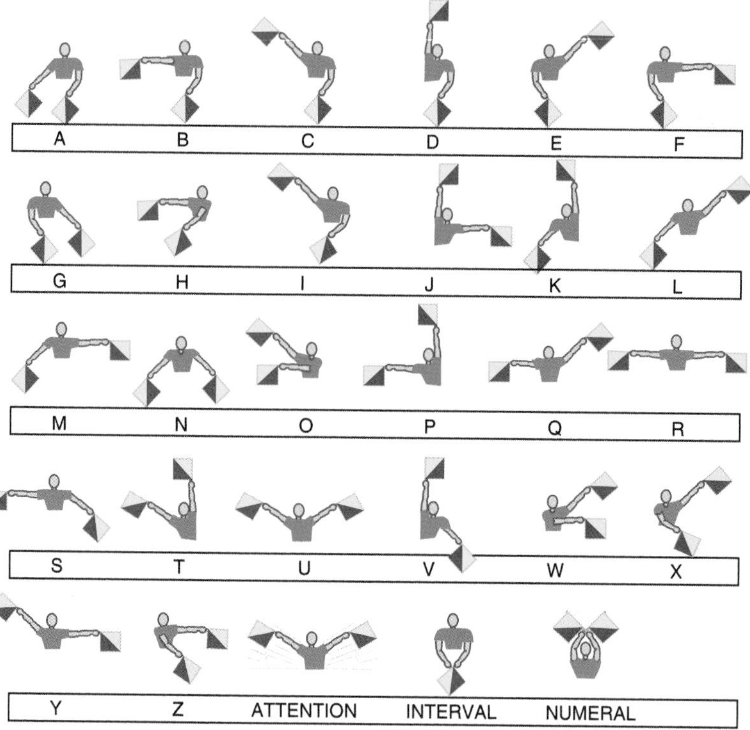

Morse Code

The telegraph was patented in 1837 by American artist ***Samuel F. B. Morse***. In its day, the telegraph was the only machine that could send instant messages across long distances. It worked by sending messages in code through electric wires. The code, known as ***Morse code***, consists of combinations of dots and dashes, which stand for the letters in the alphabet.

A	B	C	D	E	F	G
●■	■●●●	●● ●	■●●	●	●■●	■■●
H	**I**	**J**	**K**	**L**	**M**	**N**
●●●●	●●	■●■●	■●■	■	■■	■●
O	**P**	**Q**	**R**	**S**	**T**	**U**
● ●	●●●●●	●●■●	● ●●	●●●	■	●●■
V	**W**	**X**	**Y**	**Z**		
●●●■	●■■	●■●●	●● ●●	●●● ●		
&		**$**				
● ●●●		●●● ●■●●				

1	2	3	4
●■■●	●●■●●	●●●■●	●●●●■
5	**6**	**7**	**8**
■■■	●●●●●●	■■●●	■●●●●
9	**0**		
■●●■	■		
comma	**period**	**semicolon**	**question mark**
●■●■	●●■■●●	●●● ●●	■●●■●

Letter Sounds and Words

Chapter 1 Vowel and Consonant Sounds

Where Sounds Are Made

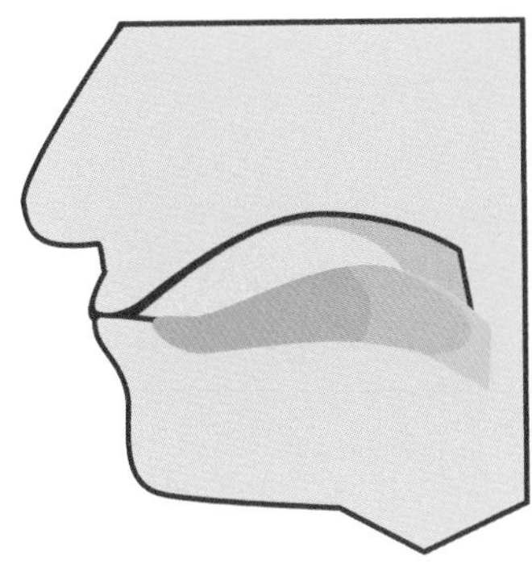

bilabial shape
(m,p,b,w)

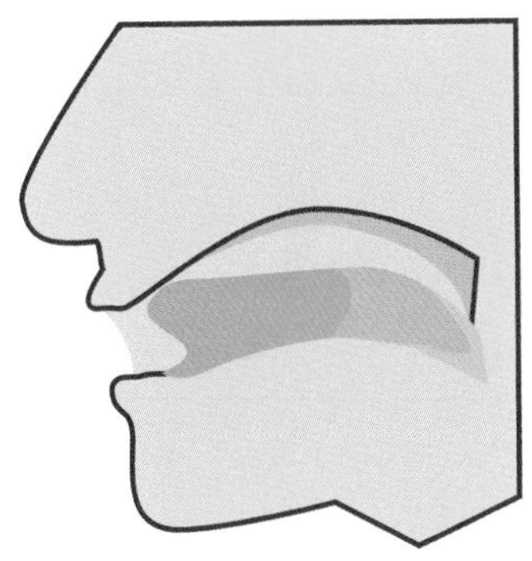

alveolar shape
(t,d,ch,j,n)

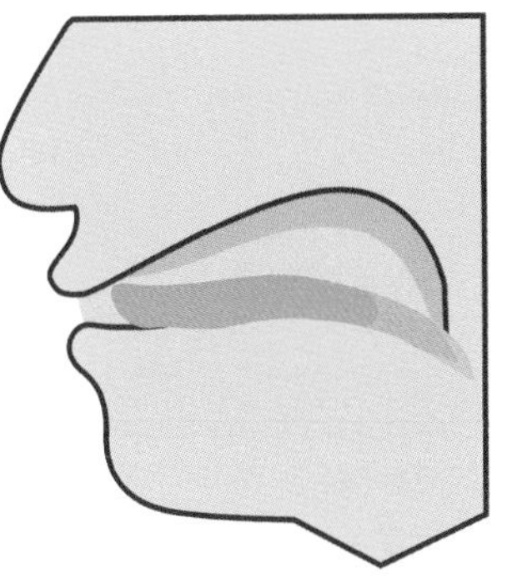

linguadental shape
(s,z,sh)

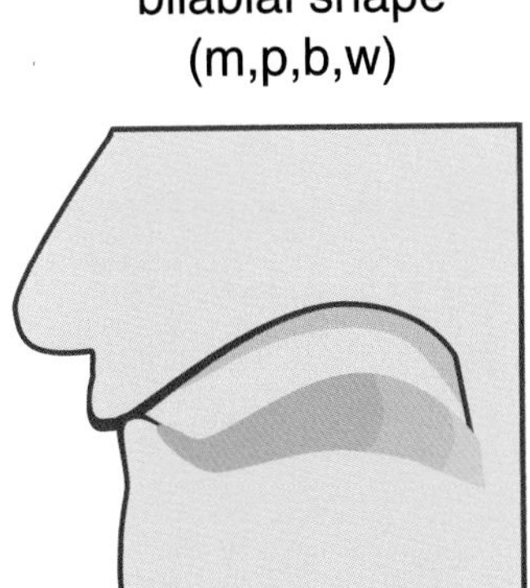

labiodental shape
(f,v)

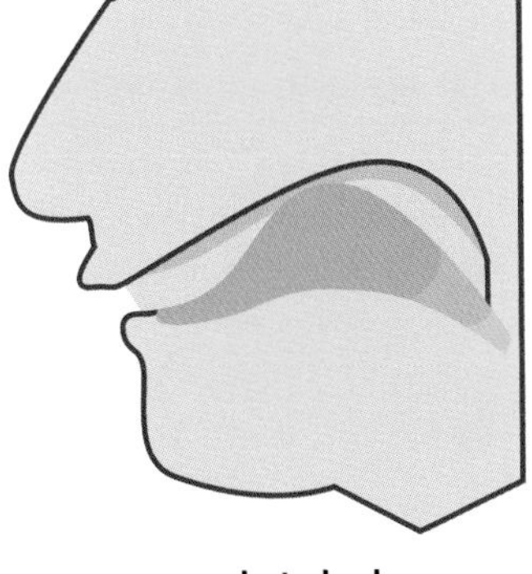

palatal shape
(y)

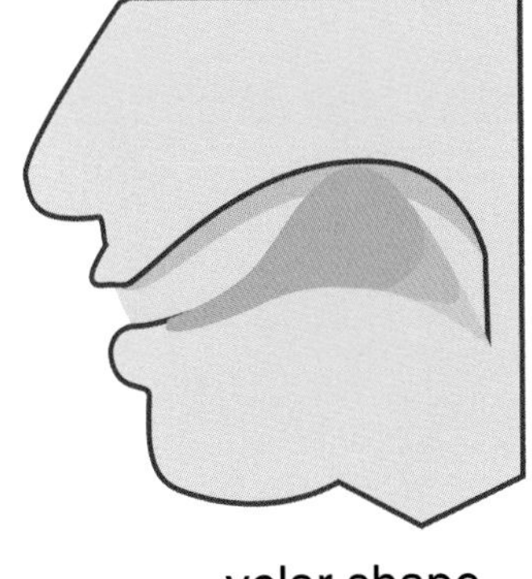

velar shape
(g,k)

Vowels and Consonants

The English alphabet is made up of 26 letters. These letters are divided into two groups: ***vowels*** and ***consonants***. There are 21 consonants

b c d f g h j k l m n p q r s t v w x y z

and five vowels

a e i o u.

The letter ***y*** sometimes serves as a vowel, for example, in the words **my, by, only,** and **symbol.**

Picture Keys to Vowel Sounds

Vowel	short		long	
a	 apple	ă	 angel	ā
e	 elephant	ĕ	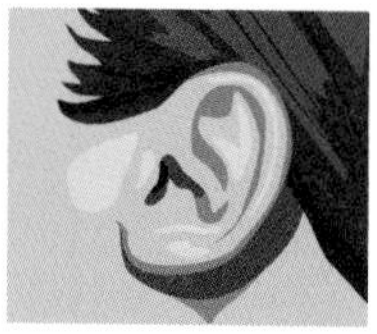 ear	ē
i	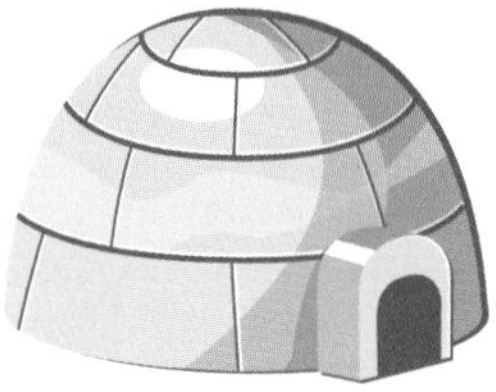 igloo	ĭ	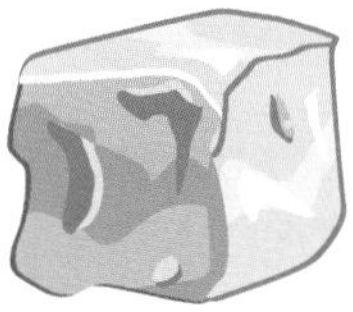 ice	ī
o	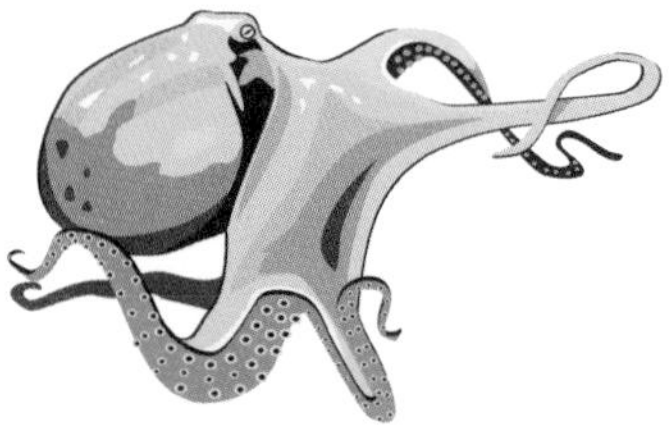 octopus	ŏ	 oak leaf	ō
u	 umbrella	ŭ	 universe	ū

Vowel Digraphs

Vowel digraphs are usually two vowels written together. Some stand for the sound of a long vowel (ai, ea, ie, oa). Others stand for special vowel sounds (oi, ou, oo, au, ew).

al, ay	**pain, say**
ea, ee	**bean, see**
ie, igh	**tie, high**
oa, oe, ow	**boat, toe, snow**
oi, oy	**boil, toy**
ou, ow	**out, cow**
oo	**boot, book (this digraph stands for two different sounds)**
au, aw	**sauce, claw**
ew, ue	**grew, blue**

Other common vowel spelling patterns:

ight	**height, night**
all	**ball**
alk, alt	**walk, salt**
ild, ind	**wild, find**
old	**told**
ear, eer	**fear, deer**

Blends

Blends are two or more consonants that keep their regular sounds when combined. Blends may appear at the beginning, middle, or end of words.

Some common beginning blends are bl, br, cl, cr, dr, fl, fr, gl, gr, pl, pr, sk, sl, sm, sn, st, and tr.

Some common ending blends are ft, mp, nd, and nt.

Sometimes when two or more consonants are written together, they stand for a new sound. These blends are called ***digraphs***.

ch, tch	**chair, match**
sh	**ship, wish**
th	**thin, that (stands for two sounds—voiced and unvoiced)**
wh	**whale**
ph	**phone**

Sometimes when two or more consonants are written together, one of the letters is silent.

kn	**know**
wr	**write**
gn	**gnat**
mb	**comb**

Voiced and Unvoiced

Sounds can be ***voiced*** or ***unvoiced***. A voiced sound is made by vibrating the vocal cords with air from the lungs. All vowels are voiced. Unvoiced sounds are made without vibrating the vocal cords, and often using the tongue and teeth. Many consonants are unvoiced.

Schwa

The ***schwa*** is the vowel sound heard in an unstressed syllable (ˊ). The symbol for schwa looks like an upside-down small *e*. Schwa sounds like a short *u* (u or uh). For example:

syllable = sil ə bə l

(See also Pronunciation Keys, p. 37.)

Accentuate the Syllable

Syllables are words or parts of words in which a vowel sound is heard. Syllables can be simple phonemes, or sounds that have no particular meaning. Syllables can also be morphemes, or sounds that have meaning. Accents tell which syllable in a word receives emphasis.
For example:

banana = ba nan´a **friendship =** friend´ ship

Sometimes more than one syllable is stressed. The louder syllable takes the ***primary accent***. The less loud stressed syllable takes the ***secondary accent***. For example:

elementary = el´ e men´ ta ry **cafeteria =** caf´ e te´ ri a

Chapter 2

Prefixes, Suffixes, and Roots

Prefixes

Prefixes are groups of letters that have meaning and are at the beginnings of words. When a prefix is attached to a word, its meaning combines with the meaning of the original word to form a new word. ***Prefix*** is a good example. ***Pre-*** comes from Latin and means "before." ***Fix*** means "to attach." So ***prefix*** means "to attach before"—in this case, to attach before a word.

COMMON GREEK AND LATIN PREFIXES

Prefix	Origin	Meaning	Example
acro-	Greek	top, high	acrobat (walker up high)
aero-	Greek	air	aerobic (using air)
alti-	Latin	high	altitude (height)
amphi-	Greek	both, around	amphibian (living in both air and water)
ana-	Greek	not, wrong	anachronism (in the wrong time frame)
andro-	Greek	man	android (robot with human features)
ante-	Latin	before	antebellum (before the war, usually the Civil War)
anthro-	Greek	man	anthropology (study of humans)
aqua-, aque-	Latin	water	aquarium (water-filled tank)
arch(i)-	Greek	chief, main	architect (building designer)
archaeo-	Greek	very old	archaeology (study of human life in the past)
arthro-	Greek	joint	arthropod (animals, usually insects, with jointed legs)
astro-	Greek	star	asteroid (star that moves through space)
atmo-	Greek	vapor, gas	atmosphere (layer of gases surrounding a planet)
audio-	Latin	sound, hearing	audiometer (instrument used to test hearing)
baro-	Greek	weight	barometer (instrument that measures air pressure)
biblio-	Greek	book	bibliography (list of books)
bio-	Greek	life, living	biology (the science of living things)
centi-	Latin	hundred	centipede (100-legged arthropod)
chloro-	Greek	green	chlorophyll (substance that makes plants green)

+

=

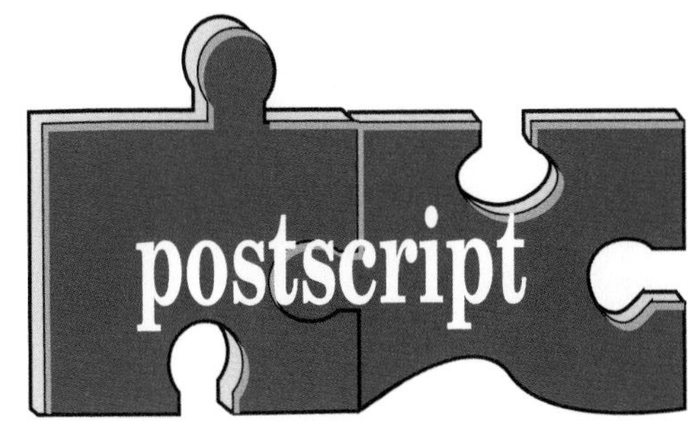

prefix + *word* = *new word*

Prefix	Origin	Meaning	Example
chrono-	Greek	time	chronology (list of events in the order in which they happened)
circum-	Latin	around	circumference (distance around a circle or sphere)
co-	Latin	together	cooperate (work together)
contra-	Latin	against	contradict (say the opposite)
cosmo-	Greek	universe	cosmic (having to do with the universe)
crypto-	Greek	hidden, secret	cryptogram (message written in code)
de-	Latin	not, put down	deny (say something is not true)
deca-	Greek	ten	decade (10 years)
deci-	Latin	tenth	decimal (based on the number 10)
denti-	Latin	tooth	dentist (tooth doctor)
di(s)-	Latin	apart	disconnect (take apart)
dia-	Greek	through	diameter (straight line that passes through the center of a circle)
digit-	Latin	finger	digits (the numbers 0 through 9; fingers and toes)
dino-	Greek	terrible	dinosaur (terrible lizard)
dyna-	Greek	force	dynamite (powerful explosive)
equi-	Latin	equal	equivalent (equal in amount, value, or meaning)
geo-	Greek	earth, land	geography (study of Earth's surface)
glosso-	Greek	tongue	glossary (list of words and their meanings)
grapho-	Greek	written, writing	graphology (study of handwriting)
helio-	Greek	sun	heliocentric (arrangement of planets with a sun in the center, as in our solar system)
hemi-	Greek	half	hemisphere (half of a sphere)
hetero-	Greek	different	heterogeneous (made up of different parts)
hexa-	Greek	six	hexagon (flat figure with six sides and six angles)
homo-	Greek	same	homophones (words that sound the same)
hydro-	Greek	water	hydroelectric (electricity coming from waterpower)
hypno-	Greek	sleep	hypnotize (to relax someone into a sleeplike condition)
il-, im-	Latin	not, against	illegal, imperfect (against the law; not perfect)
inter-	Latin	between	interplanetary (between planets)
intra-, intro-	Latin	inside	introduce (make known; bring inside)
iso-	Greek	equal	isosceles triangle (triangle with two equal sides)
magni-	Latin	great	magnificent (great in beauty, importance, or decoration)
mal(e)-	Latin	evil, bad	malice (bad feeling, wanting to do evil things to others)
mega-	Greek	great	megaphone (cone-shaped tube that, when talked through, makes the human voice louder or greater)
metro-	Greek	measure	meter (basic unit of measuring length in the metric system)

Prefix	Origin	Meaning	Example
micro-	Greek	small	microscope (instrument that makes small things appear larger)
mono-	Greek	one	monotone (unchanging tone or pitch; drone)
multi-	Latin	many	multitude (many people or things)
neo-	Greek	new	neonatal (newborn)
nocti-	Latin	night	nocturnal (active at night)
ob-	Latin	against	object (go against)
octa-	Latin	eight	octagon (flat figure with eight sides and eight angles)
omni-	Latin	all	omnivore (animal that eats both plants and animals)
ped- , pedi-	Latin	foot	pedal (foot-operated lever)
pedo- , pedi-	Greek	child	pediatrician (doctor for babies and children)
per-	Latin	thorough, complete	perfect (complete in every way)
poly-	Greek	many	polygon (flat figure with many sides)
post-	Latin	after	postscript, P.S. (note added after the signature on a letter)
pre-	Latin	before	previous (event that happened before)
pro-	Latin	for	promote (work for the growth or success of a person, idea, company, etc.)
re-	Latin	again	return (come again)
retro-	Latin	backward	retrorocket (rocket fired in the opposite direction of a larger rocket to slow it down)
rhino-	Greek	nose	rhinoceros (large mammal with one or two large horns on its snout)
sub-	Latin	below, under	submerge (put under water)
super-, supra-	Latin	above	superior (in a position above)
terra-	Latin	land	terrarium (glass tank used to grow plants or raise small land animals)
trans-	Latin	over, across, beyond	transport (carry over land, water, or through air)
ultra-	Latin	beyond	ultrasonic (having to do with sounds that are beyond the ability of humans to hear)
uni-	Latin	one	unicorn (imaginary horselike animal with one horn growing from the top of its head)

Suffixes

Suffixes, like prefixes, combine their meanings with the meaning of the words to which they are added to form new words. But suffixes are "fixed," or attached, to the ***ends*** of words.

Many suffixes change the original word from one ***part of speech*** to another. For example, the suffix ***-er*** changes the verb ***teach*** to the noun ***teacher***. The suffix ***-er*** also is used to make comparisons. My dog is ***nice*** but my cat is ***nicer***. The suffix ***-ing*** is also used to change one part of speech to another, often a verb to a noun. For example, ***teach*** to ***teaching*** (see also Gerunds, p. 55). The suffix ***-ing*** is also used to form present participles (see p. 45). Another common suffix in English is ***-ed***. It is used to form the past participles of regular verbs (see p. 45) and to form adjectives from nouns. For example, *Robin Milligan has a strong will. The strong-willed student is Robin Milligan.*

Adding Suffixes

Adding suffixes can be as simple as adding a suffix to a root word, with no changes in spelling of either the root word or the suffix. But there are some cases when the spelling of root words changes in order to receive a suffix. Following are some rules for adding suffixes to different types of root words.

Unless a root word ends in ***y***, simply add ***-ly***.

mere + ly = merely
kind + ly = kindly
bold + ly = boldly

Exceptions to this rule include:

true + ly = truly
whole + ly = wholly
simple + ly = simply

For root words that end in ***y***, change the ***y*** to ***i*** and add suffixes that begin with consonants, such as ***-ly***, ***-ness***, ***-ful***, and ***-ment***.

wary + ly = warily
naughty + ness = naughtiness
beauty + ful = beautiful
merry + ment = merriment

If a suffix begins with a consonant, it can usually be added to a root word that ends in a consonant or in a silent ***e***.

kind + ness = kindness
nice + ness = niceness
govern + ment = government
induce + ment = inducement
certain + ly = certainly
sincere + ly = sincerely
art + ful = artful
shame + ful = shameful

Exceptions to this rule include:

judgment truly wholly

If a suffix begins with a vowel— ***-ed***, ***-ing***, ***-ate***, ***-ous***, ***-ably***, ***-al***, or ***-y***—drop the silent ***e*** at the end of a root word.

hope + ed = hoped
race + ing = racing
fame + ous = famous
nature + al = natural
laze + y = lazy
fortune + ate = fortunate

Double the final consonant of a one-syllable root word that ends in a vowel followed by a consonant before adding a suffix that begins with a vowel.

bat + t + ing = batting
flip + p + ed = flipped
hot + t + er = hotter

In root words that end in ***y***, change the ***y*** to ***i*** before adding the suffixes ***-age***, ***-ly***, or ***-ness***.

carry + age = carriage
busy + ly = busily
happy + ness = happiness

COMMON GREEK AND LATIN SUFFIXES

SUFFIX	ORIGIN	MEANING	EXAMPLE
-archy	Greek	rule	monarchy (state or country ruled by a king, a queen, or an emperor)
-biosis	Greek	life	symbiosis (two or more living things that support each other)
-chrome	Greek	color	monochrome (picture presented in one color only)
-cide	Latin	kill	homicide (murder)
-cracy	Greek	form of rule	democracy (government run by people, not by a king, a queen, an emperor, or a dictator)
-derm	Greek	skin	epidermis (outer layer of skin)
-drome	Greek	running	hippodrome (arena for horse race or show)
-emia	Greek	of the blood	anemia (blood without enough red blood cells)
-fuge	Latin	away from	refuge (shelter or protection from danger)
-gamy	Greek	marriage	monogamy (marriage to one person at a time)
-geny	Greek	bearing	progeny (children)
-gon	Greek	angle	polygon (flat figure with four or more angles)
-grade	Latin	walking	centigrade (scale for measuring progressing temperature, from freezing at 0° to boiling at 100°)
-gram, -graph	Greek	writing	telegraph (message sent by a device that uses electrical wires)
-hedron	Greek	having sides	polyhedron (solid figure with many sides)
-iatrics	Greek	treatment of disease	geriatrics (medical treatment of senior citizens)
-itis	Greek	disease	arthritis (joint disease)
-lepsy	Greek	attack	narcolepsy (sudden attack of sleepiness)
-lith	Greek	made of stone	monolith (large freestanding stone)
-logy	Greek	spoken, a theory, or science	paleontology (science of prehistoric life)
-mania	Greek	type of madness	kleptomania (uncontrollable desire to steal)
-meter	Greek	instrument	thermometer (instrument used for measuring temperature)
-nomy	Greek	laws ruling	astronomy (science of outer space)
-oid	Greek	in the form of	asteroid (small bodies in space that orbit the sun)
-opia	Greek	of the eye	myopia (nearsightedness)
-ous	Latin	having the qualities of, full	beauteous (having the qualities of beauty)
-pathy	Greek	feeling, suffering	antipathy (strong feeling of dislike)
-phany	Greek	appearance	epiphany (sudden appearance of the solution to a problem, or the meaning of a phrase or sentence, etc.)
-phobia	Greek	fear, dread	claustrophobia (fear of being closed into small places)
-phone	Greek	sound	homophone (sound that is the same as another but spelled differently)

COMMON GREEK AND LATIN ROOTS

The ***root*** is the main part of a word, the part that contains the basic meaning.

ROOT	ORIGIN	MEANING	EXAMPLE
act	Latin	do	action, activity
anim	Latin	breath/spirit	animation, animal
art	Latin	skill	artistic, artisan
cardi	Latin	heart	cardiac, cardiologist
clar	Latin	clear	clarity, declare, clarification
cogn	Latin	know	recognize, cognition, incognito
cred	Latin	believe	incredible, credibility
cycle	Greek	wheel/circle	bicycle, cyclone
dent	Latin	tooth	dentist, dentures
duc/duct	Latin	convey/lead	conduct, educate
fac	Latin	make/do	factory, factor
fract/frag	Latin	break	fragment, fracture
gen	Latin	birth	generation, congenital
gram	Greek	write/letter	grammar, diagram
grat	Latin	pleasing	gratitude, grateful
imag	Latin	imitate/likeness	image, imagination
lab	Latin	work	labor, elaborate, laboratory
loc	Latin	place	location, dislocate
luna	Latin	moon	lunar, lunatic
man	Latin	hand	manual, manuscript
mand	Latin	to order	mandatory, command
max	Latin	most	maximum
merge	Latin	dip/dive	submerge, emerge
meter	Greek	measure	millimeter, thermometer
mob	Latin	move	mobile, automobile
mort	Latin	death	mortal, mortify
mov	Latin	move	movie, remove

ROOT	ORIGIN	MEANING	EXAMPLE
narr	Latin	tell	narrate
nav	Latin	ship	navigator, naval
neg	Latin	no	negative, negate
nov	Latin	new	innovation, novel
opt	Latin	best	optimal, optimize
pater	Latin	father	paternal, patriarch
port	Latin	carry	portable, import, deport
psych	Greek	mind/soul	psychiatry, psychic
put	Latin	thing	compute, putative, dispute
san	Latin	health	sanitary, sane
sci	Latin	know	conscious, science
sol	Latin	alone	solo, solitary
spec	Latin	see/look	spectator, speculate
sphere	Latin	ball	hemisphere, atmosphere
sum	Latin	highest	summate, summary
temp	Latin	time	tempo, comtemporary
term	Latin	end	terminal, determine
terr	Latin	land/earth	terrain, territory
therm	Greek	heat	thermal, thermometer
tox	Greek	poison	toxic, toxin
urb	Latin	city	urban, urbane, suburb
vac	Latin	empty	vacuum, vacant, evacuate
vid/vis	Latin	see	video, vision
voc	Greek	voice	vocation, invoke

Spelling Sounds and Words

Five Basic Rules for Spelling

1 Words containing ie or ei

I before ***e***, except after ***c***, or when sounding like ***a***, as in ***neighbor*** and ***weigh***.

I before E		Except after C	Sounding as A
die	grief	ceiling	sleigh
lie	chief	receipt	vein
tie	believe	deceive	eight

Exceptions to the "i before e" rule include ceiling, conceit, either, foreign, height, leisure, neither, sheik, species, and weird.

2 Silent or final e

If a word ends with a silent ***e***, drop the ***e*** before adding a suffix that begins with a vowel.

bore/boring ***love/loving*** ***skate/skating***

Do not drop the silent ***e*** before adding a suffix that begins with a consonant.

bore/boredom ***hate/hateful*** ***skate/skateboard***

Exceptions to the "silent e" rule include argument, ninth, and truly.

3 Final y

If a word ends in a consonant followed by ***y***, change the ***y*** to ***i*** before adding a suffix.

cry/cried ***friendly/friendliness*** ***gloomy/gloominess***

If a word ends in ***y*** with a vowel before it, do not change ***y*** to ***i*** before adding suffixes or other endings.

destroy/destroyed ***play/playing*** ***volley/volleys***

If a suffix begins with i, do not change the y, for example: crying, dryish.

4 Consonant preceded by a vowel

If a one-syllable word ends with one consonant with a vowel before it, double the final consonant before adding a suffix.

can/canned ***nut/nutty*** ***pot/pottery***

If a multisyllable word ends with a consonant preceded by a vowel and the accent is on the last syllable, double the final consonant before adding a suffix.

acquit/acquittal ***control/controlling*** ***repel/repellent***

If a word with more than one syllable ends in a consonant preceded by a vowel but the last syllable is unaccented, do not double the consonant before adding a suffix, for example: travel/traveler, honor/honorable, and widen/widened.

5 One-plus-one rule

When a prefix ends in the same letter with which the main word begins, include both of the repeated letters.

il- + logical = illogical ***mis- + spell = misspell***

When a suffix begins with the same letter with which a main word ends, include both the repeated letters.

accidental + ly = accidentally ***mean + ness = meanness***

The one-plus-one rule also applies to making compound words. Include all letters of both words, even if they are repeated.

room + mate = roommate

Commonly Mispelled Words

accessory
accompany
acquaintance
acquire
address
all right
a lot
already
Antarctic
arithmetic
asthma
athlete
available
banana
bargain
beauty
believe
broccoli
calendar
cantaloupe
caterpillar
ceiling
cemetery
chief
cinnamon
committee
congratulations
conscience
conscious
corduroy
cough
counterfeit
debt
definite
dependent
desperate
diarrhea
disappear
dumb
eighth
environment
exaggerate
exceed
excel
exercise
exist
fascinate
February
forehead
formally
formerly
freight
gauge
glacier
government
grammar
guarantee
guess
guest
handkerchief
height
independence
judgment
kindergarten
laugh
league
library
license
literature
maintenance
mathematics
mattress
misspell
mosquitoes
necessary
neighbor
niece
noticeable
nuisance
obedience
occurred
omitted
parallel
plaid
potatoes
prairie
privilege
probably
raspberry
receipt
reference
relieve
rhythm
ridiculous
sandwich
scissors
separately
special
squirrel
tomatoes
truly
Tuesday
usually
vaccinate
vacuum
Wednesday

Homophones, Homonyms, and Homographs

Homophones are sounds that are the same but are spelled differently. For example, ***f*** and ***ph*** are often used to spell the same sound, as in:

fine or file and phone or physical

C and ***s*** can also spell the same sound, as in:

circus or cereal and symbol or sign

And ***g*** and ***j*** can also spell the same sound, as in:

refuge or sergeant and jump or jinx

The word ***homophone*** comes from the Greek words ***homo*** (same) and ***phone*** (sound). It is also used to describe ***homonyms***, or words that sound the same but have different meanings. The word ***homonym*** also comes from Greek words ***homo*** and ***onyma*** (name). (See also The Secret of Nyms, p. 36.)

> **Homonyms that not only sound the same but are also spelled the same are called *homographs*. The word *homograph* comes from the Greek words *homo* and *graph*, which mean "same writing" (see Prefixes, Suffixes, and Roots, pp. 19–25).**

Please mail this letter.
The letter came in the mail.
The knight wore armor and chain mail.

We wore our swimsuits to the pool.
Mom drives to work in a car pool.
I have a pool table in my basement.

Familiar Homonyms

allowed/aloud	I was ***allowed*** to play my stereo after school. We read ***aloud*** in class.
ant/aunt	The ***ant*** is a frequent visitor at picnics. My ***aunt*** is my father's sister.
ate/eight	I ***ate*** lunch at school last week. I have ***eight*** video games.
bare/bear	Don't walk outside in your ***bare*** feet. The ***bear*** lives in the woods.
berry/bury	The ***berry*** from that bush is poisonous. The squirrel tried to ***bury*** the acorn.
blew/blue	The storm ***blew*** in from the west. ***Blue*** is my favorite color.
brake/break	I had to ***brake*** to slow down my bicycle. I didn't mean to ***break*** the glass vase.
capital/capitol	Please remember where to use ***capital*** letters. We met Senator Smith in the ***capitol*** building.
cent/scent/sent	I don't have a ***cent*** to my name! That perfume has an awful ***scent***. I ***sent*** a letter to my best friend.
colonel/kernel	The ***colonel*** led the soldiers in battle. I found only one unpopped ***kernel*** in the popcorn bowl.
dear/deer	My puppy is very ***dear*** to me. I saw some ***deer*** at the petting zoo.
fair/fare	The weather is ***fair*** today. I paid full ***fare*** for my airplane ticket.
feat/feet	The acrobat performed a breathtaking ***feat*** on the high wire. My ***feet*** hurt from standing too long.
flew/flu/flue	The birds ***flew*** past my window. I had the ***flu*** over spring vacation. The smoke and ash rose up the chimney ***flue***.
flour/flower	We'll need some ***flour*** to make the pancake batter. The violet is our state ***flower***.
heal/heel/he'll	That scratch should ***heal*** quickly. My new shoes rubbed a blister on my ***heel***. ***He'll*** be coming 'round the mountain when he comes.

hear/here	Please speak louder because I can't ***hear*** you. Come over ***here***!
heard/herd	I ***heard*** the news on the radio. A ***herd*** of cattle moves to the lower pasture every afternoon.
hole/whole	My dog dug a ***hole*** in the backyard. I read the ***whole*** book in one morning.
hour/our	I'll be ready in one ***hour***. ***Our*** next meeting is in one month.
know/no	I didn't ***know*** half the answers on the quiz. ***No***, I don't think I passed.
loan/lone	She asked him to ***loan*** her money for lunch. When the other frogs left, Ribbet was the ***lone*** frog in the pond.
mail/male	I put the letter in the ***mail*** yesterday. It was an all-***male*** club and no girls could join.
main/mane	I think I understand the ***main*** idea of the story. That male lion has a thick, beautiful ***mane***.
meat/meet	I'm vegetarian now, so I don't eat ***meat***. ***Meet*** me at the mall at seven o'clock.
one/won	Give me ***one*** good reason for going to study hall. Our team ***won*** at the science fair.
pail/pale	I took my little sister's ***pail*** and shovel to the beach. Your face went ***pale*** when your name was called.
pain/pane	Cleaning my room is a real ***pain***. The window was made of one large ***pane*** of glass.
pair/pear	I have one ***pair*** of jeans. The apple looks tastier than the ***pear***.
peace/piece	The two countries signed a ***peace*** treaty. I had a ***piece*** of that delicious chocolate cake.
plain/plane	The skirt was ***plain***, but the blouse was fancy. We flew on a ***plane*** to visit my grandfather.
pray/prey	Let's ***pray*** for good weather for our field trip. Eagles and owls are birds of ***prey***.
principal/principle	The ***principal*** idea of the story is that people should get along. My teacher is a person of ***principle***.
rain/reign/rein	The ***rain*** fell for two days before the sun came out again. The queen's ***reign*** won't end until she dies. She told me to take the horse by the ***reins***.
right/write	Turn ***right*** at the corner. ***Write*** a letter to your uncle.
role/roll	I auditioned for a ***role*** in the school play. My favorite lunch is peanut butter and jelly on a ***roll***.
sail/sale	The captain and crew set ***sail*** in their three-masted ship. My mother says I can't get the jacket until it's on ***sale***.

scene/seen	She painted a forest ***scene*** in art class. I haven't ***seen*** her since three o'clock.
soar/sore	Did you see the eagle ***soar*** through the sky? Throwing the ball made the new pitcher's arm ***sore***.
some/sum	Have ***some*** pie if you're hungry. The ***sum*** of two and two is four.
son/sun	The father had one ***son*** and three daughters. The ***sun*** rises in the east.
stair/stare	It took the baby a long time to climb each ***stair***. Looking around is fine, but please don't ***stare***.
stationary/stationery	The statue is ***stationary*** so you can't move it. Use nice ***stationery*** for writing thank-you notes.
steal/steel	He used to ***steal*** pennies from his sister's piggy bank. The car body is made of ***steel***.
suite/sweet	The ***suite*** of rooms was decorated in blue and green. The lemonade was too ***sweet***.
tail/tale	My dog has a very long ***tail***. Did you read the ***tale*** of Paul Bunyan and Babe, the blue ox?
their/there/they're	***Their*** house is on the next block. Her dog is ***there***, behind the fence. ***They're*** going to be happy after the quiz.
threw/through	She ***threw*** the ball past home plate. The ball flew ***through*** the air.
to/too/two	I went ***to*** the dance. My friend came, ***too***. The ***two*** of us danced together.
waist/waste	I like my belt around my hips, not my ***waist***. Don't ***waste*** that perfectly good paper.
wait/weight	Please ***wait*** for me. I'd guess your ***weight*** to be about 70 pounds.
way/weigh	Let's take the back ***way*** home. How many pounds do you ***weigh***?
weak/week	She grew thin and ***weak*** from her illness. It took one ***week*** to recover.
wear/where	I thought I'd ***wear*** cutoffs to camp. ***Where*** did I put my homework?
weather/whether	The ***weather*** was warm and sunny. I don't know ***whether*** I should go or not.
which/witch	***Which*** witch is ***which***? The ***witch*** knew hundreds of spells.

PALINDROMES SEMORDNILAP

mom

dad

noon

level

radar

Palindromes are words, phrases, and sentences that read the same way forward and backward!

Madam, I'm Adam.

Able was I ere I saw Elba.

A man. A plan. A canal: Panama.

Rats live on no evil star.

Abbreviations

Abbreviations are shortened forms of words. They are made by leaving letters out or by replacing a group of letters with another letter or symbol.

AC	alternating current (type of electrical current)
A.D.	anno Domini (Latin for "in the year of the Lord," or since the birth of Christ)
a.m.	ante meridiem (from midnight until noon)
asap	as soon as possible
A.S.P.C.A.	American Society for the Prevention of Cruelty to Animals
BA	Bachelor of Arts (college degree)
B.C.	before Christ
B.C.E.	before the Christian era
BS	Bachelor of Science
C	centigrade or Celsius
c.	copyright or circa
CIA	Central Intelligence Agency
cm	centimeter
COD	cash on delivery
CPA	certified public accountant
CPR	cardiopulmonary resuscitation
DA	district attorney
DC	direct current (type of electrical current)
D.C.	District of Columbia
DDS	doctor of dental surgery
DNA	deoxyribonucleic acid (the basic material of genes)
DOA	dead on arrival
ed.	editor, edition
ESP	extrasensory perception

esp.	especially
et al.	et alia (and others)
etc.	et cetera (and so forth)
F	Fahrenheit (scale for measuring temperature)
FBI	Federal Bureau of Investigation
FYI	for your information
GOP	Grand Old Party (Republican party)
Hon.	the Honorable
HRH	His Royal Highness, Her Royal Highness
ie	id est (that is)
IQ	intelligence quotient
IRS	Internal Revenue Service
K	1,000
k.	karat (unit of weight)
kg	kilogram
km	kilometer
l	liter
l.	latitude
lb.	*libra* (pound)
MD	*medicinae doctor* (doctor of medicine)
mfg.	manufacturing
ml	milliliter
mm	millimeter
mph	miles per hour
ms.	manuscript
MSG	monosodium glutamate (flavor enhancer)
NAACP	National Association for the Advancement of Colored People
no.	number
oz.	ounce
p.	page
p.m.	post meridiem (from noon until midnight)
P.S.	postscript
pt.	pint
qt.	quart
RFD	rural free delivery (U.S. mail category)
RIP	rest in peace
RN	registered nurse
RR	railroad
RSVP	*répondez s'il vous plaît* (French for please respond)
SASE	self-addressed, stamped envelope
St.	street, saint
t.	ton
TNT	trinitrotoluene (an explosive)
UFO	unidentified flying object
UHF	ultrahigh frequency (radio waves)
v. or vs.	versus (against)
VCR	videocassette recorder
VHF	very high frequency (radio waves)
w	watt (unit for measuring electrical power)

Contractions

A ***contraction*** is formed by putting together two words with certain letters left out. An ***apostrophe*** (**'**) is used in place of the missing letters.

aren't	are not
can't	cannot
couldn't	could not
could've	could have
didn't	did not
doesn't	does not
don't	do not
hadn't	had not
hasn't	has not
haven't	have not
he'd	he had/he would
he'll	he will
he's	he is
I'm	I am
isn't	is not
it'd	it had/it would
it'll	it will
it's	it is
let's	let us
mightn't	might not
might've	might have
mustn't	must not
she'd	she had/she would
she'll	she will
she's	she is
shouldn't	should not
should've	should have
there'd	there had/there would
there'll	there will
there's	there is
they'll	they will
they're	they are
'twas	it was
wasn't	was not
we'll	we will
we're	we are
weren't	were not
what'd	what had/what would
what's	what is
won't	will not
wouldn't	would not
would've	would have
you'll	you will
you're	you are

Using the Dictionary

Chapter 1 The Parts of a Dictionary

Guide words usually appear in the outer corner of each page of a dictionary. The first guide word identifies the first main entry on the page. The second word identifies the last word on the page.

New letters break the dictionary into different sections, based on alphabetical order.

Pronunciation of the main entry follows the entry word or words.

Main entry word or words are usually set in bold type.

Variations in spelling follow the preferred spelling of the main entry.

Illustrations are used to add visual reinforcement to written definitions.

rabbi ▸ racquetball

rab·bi (rab-eye) ***noun*** A Jewish religious leader and teacher.

rab·bit (rab-it) ***noun*** A small, furry mammal with long ears that lives in a hole that it digs in the ground. *See* **angora.**

rab·ble (rab-uhl) ***noun*** A noisy crowd of people.

ra·bies (ray-beez) ***noun*** An often fatal disease that can affect humans, dogs, bats, and other warm-blooded animals. Rabies is caused by a virus that attacks the brain and spinal cord and is spread by the bite of an infected animal.
▷ ***adjective*** **rabid** (rab-id)

rac·coon (ra-koon) ***noun*** A mammal with rings on its tail and black and white face markings that look like a mask.

race (rayss)
1. *noun* A test of speed. ▷ ***verb*** **race**
2. *noun* One of the major groups into which human beings can be divided. People of the same race share the same physical characteristics, such as skin color, which are passed on from generation to generation.
3. *verb* To run or move very fast. *Angela raced down the hall to get to her next class.*
▷ **racing, raced**

race car ***noun*** A car designed to race at very high speeds. *The picture shows a Ford Formula 1 race car.*

R

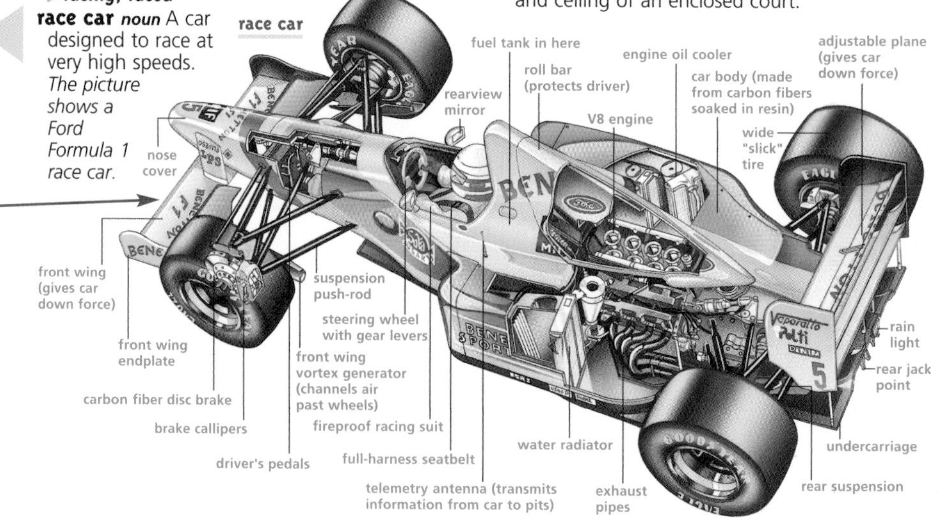

race relations ***noun, plural*** The way that people of different races get along with each other when they live in the same community.

race·track (rayss-*trak*) ***noun*** A round or oval course that is used for racing.

ra·cial (ray-shuhl) ***adjective***
1. To do with a person's race, as in *racial characteristics.*
2. Between races, as in *racial prejudice* or *racial harmony.*

rac·ist (ray-sist) ***adjective*** Someone who is **racist** thinks that a particular race is better than others or treats people unfairly or cruelly because of their race. ▷ ***noun*** **racism,** ***noun*** **racist**

rack (rak)
1. *noun* A framework for holding or hanging things, as in *a clothes rack.*
2. *noun* An instrument of torture used in the past to stretch the body of a victim.
3. *verb* If you **rack your brains,** you think very hard. *I racked my brains to remember his name.*
▷ **racking, racked**

rack·et (rak-it) ***noun***
1. racket *or* **racquet** A stringed frame with a handle that you use in games such as tennis, squash, and badminton. *See* **badminton.**
2. A very loud noise.
3. A dishonest activity. *The police exposed a gambling racket.*

rac·quet (rak-it) *See* **racket.**

rac·quet·ball (rak-it-*bawl*) ***noun*** A game played by two or four players who use short rackets to hit a small rubber ball against the walls, floor, and ceiling of an enclosed court.

426

Parts of speech are defined for each main entry or subentry.

ra·dar (ray-dar) ***noun***
1. Planes and ships use **radar** to find solid objects by reflecting radio waves off them and by receiving the reflected waves. Radar stands for *RAdio Detecting And Ranging.*
2. radar trap A system using radar equipment that is set up by the police to catch speeding drivers.

ra·di·al (ray-dee-uhl) ***adjective***
1. Spreading out from the center or arranged like rays.
2. To do with a kind of automobile or truck tire whose design makes it grip the road better than traditional tires. ▷ ***noun*** **radial**

ra·di·ant (ray-dee-uhnt) ***adjective***
1. Bright and shining.
2. Someone who is **radiant** looks very healthy and happy.
▷ ***noun*** **radiance**

ra·di·ate (ray-dee-*ate*) ***verb***
1. To give off rays of light or heat.
2. To spread out from the center.
3. To send out something strongly. *Mario radiates confidence.*
▷ ***verb*** **radiating, radiated**

ra·di·a·tion (*ray*-dee-ay-shuhn) ***noun***
1. The sending out of rays of light, heat, etc.
2. Particles that are sent out from a radioactive substance.

ra·di·a·tor (ray-dee-*ay*-tur) ***noun***
1. A metal container through which hot liquid or steam circulates, sending heat into a room.
2. A metal device through which a liquid, usually water, circulates to cool a vehicle's engine. *See* **car, race car.**

rad·i·cal (rad-i-kuhl) ***adjective***
1. If a change is **radical,** it is thorough and has a wide range of important effects. ▷ ***adverb*** **radically**
2. Someone who is **radical** believes in extreme political change. ▷ ***noun*** **radical**

ra·di·o (ray-dee-oh)
1. ***noun*** A way of communicating using electromagnetic waves broadcast from a central antenna.
2. ***noun*** A device that sends or receives these broadcasts and converts them into sound.
3. ***verb*** To send a message using a radio.
▷ **radios, radioing, radioed**
▷ ***noun, plural*** **radios** ▷ ***adjective*** **radio**

ra·di·o·ac·tive (*ray*-dee-oh-ak-tiv) ***adjective*** **Radioactive** materials are made up of atoms whose nuclei break down, giving off harmful radiation. ▷ ***noun*** **radioactivity**

ra·di·og·ra·phy (*ray*-dee-og-ruh-fee) ***noun*** The process of taking X-ray photographs of people's bones, organs, etc. ▷ ***noun*** **radiographer**

rad·ish (rad-ish) ***noun*** A small, red and white root vegetable that you eat in salads. *See* **vegetable.**
▷ ***noun, plural*** **radishes**

ra·di·um (ray-dee-uhm) ***noun*** A radioactive element sometimes used to treat cancer.

ra·di·us (ray-dee-uhss) ***noun***
1. A straight line segment drawn from the center of a circle to its outer edge. *See* **circle.**
2. The outer bone in your lower arm. *See* **skeleton.**
3. A circular area around a thing or a place. *Most of my friends live within a radius of one mile from my house.*
▷ ***noun, plural*** **radii** (ray-dee-eye)

ra·don (ray-don) ***noun*** An odorless, colorless, radioactive gas that can seep up from the earth and rocks. Radon is a chemical element produced by radium.

raf·fle (raf-uhl) ***noun*** A way of raising money by selling tickets and then giving prizes to people with winning tickets. ▷ ***verb*** **raffle**

raft (raft)
1. ***noun*** A floating platform often made from logs tied together.
2. ***verb*** To travel by raft. ▷ **rafting, rafted** ▷ ***noun*** **rafting**
3. ***noun*** An inflatable rubber craft with a flat bottom. *The picture shows an inflatable raft traveling through fast-moving water.*

inflatable raft

rag (rag)
1. ***noun*** A piece of old cloth.
2. rags ***noun, plural*** Very old, worn-out clothing.

rage (rayj)
1. ***noun*** Violent anger.
2. ***verb*** To be violent or noisy. *The wind raged around the house.* ▷ **raging, raged**

rag·ged (rag-id) ***adjective*** Old, torn, and worn-out. ▷ ***adjective*** **raggedy** ▷ ***adverb*** **raggedly**

rag·time (rag-*time*) ***noun*** An early style of jazz having a strong, syncopated rhythm.

rag·weed (rag-*weed*) ***noun*** A weed whose pollen is a cause of hay fever in the fall.

R

427

Word divisions are shown in the main entry for words of one or more syllables.

Definitions of the main entry follow the listing of pronunciation and part of speech. Definitions tell the meaning of the main entry.

Multiple definitions are provided for words with more than one meaning. The most frequently used meaning of the main entry is defined first, followed in order to the least used meaning.

Chapter 2 Dictionary Notations

Synonyms and Antonyms

synonyms: able/strong
Pearl is an ***able*** athlete and as ***strong*** as any member of the team.

antonyms: able/weak
She is an ***able*** student, although her eyes are so ***weak*** she must wear thick glasses.

synonyms: absent/elsewhere
The principal was ***absent*** because she was needed ***elsewhere***.

antonyms: absent/present
Marcia was ***absent*** today, but her brother was ***present*** for roll call.

synonyms: add/sum up
I'll ***add*** the list and then you ***sum up*** to double-check me.

antonyms: add/subtract
When you ***add*** the bill, please ***subtract*** the credit for the CDs I returned.

THE SECRET OF NYMS
Synonyms and Antonyms

What is the secret of ***nym***? Well, the secret is revealed in ***morphemics***, the study of the meanings of units of sound (see also p. 5).

First, consider ***nym***. ***Nym*** comes from the Greek ***onoma***, meaning "name."

Next, consider the Greek words ***ant*** and ***syn***. ***Ant*** means "opposite." ***Syn*** means "like" or "same."

Now, put ***nym*** together with the other words:

Ant + (o)nym = antonym — **A word of opposite meaning**

Syn + (o)nym = synonym — **A word of similar or like meaning**

You've now discovered the secret of nym!

Chapter 3 Pronunciation Keys

Vowels

a *or* ă	pat
ä *or* ah	father
ā *or* ay *or* a‿e	say, paid, fate
â(r)	air, dare
ar	barn
aw *or* ô	raw, ball
e *or* ĕ	men
ē *or* ee	seem
ēr *or* ihr	fear
i *or* ĭ	sit
ī *or* eye	icon (eye-kon), rye, tire
o *or* ŏ	hot
ō *or* oh	toe, tote
ô *or* or	more
oi	oil
o͝o	book
o͞o	ooze
ou	out
oor	poor
ou	out, now
u *or* ŭ	put
û(r) *or* ur	burn
uh	runt, comma
ə *or* uh	alone, cover, easily, scallop, minus

Consonants

b	bin, cabin, cab
ch	child
d	do, gladden, bad
f	foe
g	go
h	ham, behave
j	jet, reject, fudge
k	kick, call
l *or* ll	let, will, marshmallow bundle
m	man, summer, him
n	no, banner, on
p	pin, super, sip
r	run, flurry, steer
s *or* ss	sit, misses, pass, pace
sh	show, fashion, bash
t	ten, button, sent
th *or* TH	thin, ether, with this, wither
v	van, river, rove
w	will, away
wh	whale, which, nowhere
y	yes, onion
z	zoom, lazy, those
zh	measure, mirage

Acronyms

Acronyms are words formed from the first letters or syllables of words in phrases or titles. They are related to ***abbreviations*** (see pp. 31–32), the shortened versions of words or phrases. ***Acronyms*** don't end with periods, and are usually written in all capital letters.

AIDS	Acquired Immune Deficiency Syndrome (disease)
BASIC	Beginner's All-purpose Symbolic Instruction Code (computer language)
CARE	Citizens for American Relief Everywhere (a relief organization)
CAT scan	Computerized Axial Tomography (medical test)
DOS	Disk Operating System (computer operation program)
EPCOT	Experimental Prototype Community of Tomorrow
FICA	Federal Insurance Contributions Act (Social Security)
GATT	General Agreement on Tariffs and Trade
LASER	Light Amplification by Stimulated Emission of Radiation
loran	long-range aid to navigation (navigation tool)
MADD	Mothers Against Drunk Driving (organization to prevent drunk driving accidents)
NASA	National Aeronautics and Space Administration (U.S. space agency)
NATO	North Atlantic Treaty Organization (peacekeeping agency)
NOW	National Organization for Women
OPEC	Organization of Petroleum Exporting Countries
PIN	Personal Identification Number (used for bank cards, credit cards, etc.)
radar	Radio Detecting And Ranging (navigation device)
RAM	Random-Access Memory (short-term computer memory)
ROM	Read-Only Memory (built-in computer memory)
SADD	Students Against Drunk Driving (organization to prevent drunk driving accidents)
UNICEF	United Nations International Children's Emergency Fund (relief organization)
VISTA	Volunteers In Service To America (helping organization)
WHO	World Health Organization
ZIP code	Zone Improvement Plan (post office delivery code)

Parts of Speech

Chapter 1 Nouns

Nouns are words that name people, places, or things. Nouns come in many forms.

Common and Proper Nouns

Common nouns are general names for people, places, and things.

backpack, friend, holiday, mall, school, teacher, video

Proper nouns are names for specific people, places, and things. Proper nouns always begin with a capital letter.

E. T.	**Mrs. Johnson**
Jackson School	**Nintendo®**
Jenny	**Oakdale**
Labor Day	**Saturday**

Three little words—*a*, *an*, and *the*—mark the presence of nouns. These words are called articles. Articles are either *definite* or *indefinite*. The definite article, *the*, refers to specific or known things. The indefinite articles, *a* and *an*, refer to unspecific nouns. For example, if you are about to go on a trip, your mom will tell you to get into *the* car. Of course she means your family's car. If your older sister wants *a* big 16th birthday present, she might ask your parents for a car. This means any car, as long as it's hers.

Concrete and Abstract Nouns

Concrete nouns name people, places, and things that you can see, touch, taste, hear, or smell.

fire, library, music, perfume, pizza, snow, woman

Abstract nouns name ideas, feelings, or qualities.

beauty, democracy, fairness, health, kindness, love, sadness

Collective Nouns

Collective nouns name groups of people, places, or things.

class, club, committee, humankind, orchestra

Compound Nouns

Compound nouns are made up of two or more words. Compound nouns can be ***common***, ***proper***, ***singular***, ***plural***, ***concrete***, ***abstract***, or ***collective***. They can be one word, two words, or hyphenated.

baseball, daydreams, electric guitar, jack-o'-lantern

Singular and Plural Nouns

Singular nouns name only one person, place, or thing. ***Plural*** nouns name more than one person, place, or thing.

Possessive Nouns

A ***possessive*** noun tells who or what owns something.

The girl's desk was messy. **Jeff's ball is new.**

To make singular nouns possessive, add ***'s*** to the end of most nouns.

cat **the cat's toy**
Robert **Robert's spelling test**
Tess **Tess's notebook**

To make plural nouns possessive, add an apostrophe (***'***) to the end of the noun when the plural noun ends in ***s***.

cats **the cats' scratching posts**
students **the students' music teacher**
teachers **the teachers' lounge**

If the last letter of the plural noun does not end in ***s***, add ***'s*** to form the plural possessive.

children **the children's toys**
people **the people's choice**
geese **the geese's flight pattern**

Making a Singular Noun Plural

1. Add an ***-s*** to the end of most singular nouns to make them plural.
   dog + s = dogs **cat + s = cats** **test + s = tests**
2. Add ***-es*** to the end of a singular noun ending in ***ch***, ***s***, ***sch***, ***sh***, ***x***, or ***z*** to make it plural.
   dress + es = dresses **lunch + es = lunches** **quiz + es = quizzes**
3. Change ***f*** to ***v*** and add ***-es*** to the end of most singular nouns ending in ***f***, ***lf***, or ***fe*** to make them plural. There are exceptions to this rule!
   knife/knives **leaf/leaves** **life/lives**
   exceptions: **sniff/sniffs** **safe/safes**
4. Drop the ***y*** and add ***-ies*** to a singular noun ending in a consonant followed by ***y*** to make it plural.
   fly/flies **battery/batteries** **penny/pennies**
5. Add an ***-s*** to a singular noun ending in a vowel followed by ***y*** to make it plural.
   day/days **key/keys** **boy/boys**
6. Add ***-es*** to most words ending in ***o*** preceded by a consonant to make them plural.
   potato/potatoes **echo/echoes** **tomato/tomatoes**
7. Add an ***-s*** after the most important word in a hyphenated compound noun or to one written as two words to make it plural.
   brother-in-law/brothers-in-law **computer drive/computer drives**
8. Memorize odd plurals.
   man/men **woman/women** **goose/geese** **foot/feet**

Chapter 2 Pronouns

Pronouns are words that can be substituted for nouns in naming people, places, and things.

Personal and Possessive Pronouns

Personal pronouns refer to people or animals.

I, you, he, she, it, we, they, me, him, her, us, them

They told us that they were going to meet her at the mall.

Sometimes personal pronouns are used to show possession or ownership. These personal pronouns are sometimes called ***possessive pronouns.***

my, mine, your(s), his, her(s), its, our(s), their(s), whose

If this bubble gum isn't hers, then it must be mine.

Never use an apostrophe in a possessive pronoun!

SUBJECT PRONOUNS

Subject pronouns are often used with a noun or another pronoun as part of the subject of a clause or sentence (see pp. 56–59).

These and those are very different.

She and I went to the movies last Saturday.

Some had a great time at the party. Others did not.

OBJECT PRONOUNS

Object or ***predicate pronouns*** are often used with a noun or another pronoun as part of the direct object (see Subjects and Predicates, p. 56).

Fred saw him at the fair.

We share the dog. It belongs to her and me.

Always speak of yourself last.

Demonstrative Pronouns

Demonstrative pronouns refer to specific people, places, or things.

this, that, these, those

Which ice skates are lighter, these or those?

Indefinite Pronouns

Indefinite pronouns refer to or replace nouns in a general way. Some indefinite pronouns are also used as adjectives. They are then followed by a noun, as in ***both cats*** or ***each flower***. Examples follow:

all, any, anyone, both, each, either, every, many, neither, nobody, no one, nothing, other(s), several, some, someone.

Anyone can try out for the team, but only some will make it.

Reflexive Pronouns

Reflexive pronouns are used to refer back to subject nouns and pronouns.

myself, yourself, himself, herself, itself, ourselves, yourselves, themselves

Cathy knew she could do it herself.

Intensive Pronouns

Intensive pronouns are reflexive pronouns that emphasize a noun or another pronoun.

John himself, she herself, the team themselves

We ourselves formed the new reading club.

Interrogative Pronouns

Interrogative pronouns are pronouns used to ask questions.

what, which, who, whom, whose

What is happening and to whom?

Verbs

Verbs are words that describe an action or a state of being.

Action and Linking Verbs

Action verbs describe activity. Action can be physical.

eat, leap, read, run, sleep, swim, walk, yell

Abe Lincoln walked seven miles to school every day.

Action can also mean quieter activities.

care, concentrate, forgive, grow, hate, love, think

A tree grows in Brooklyn.

Linking verbs do not describe an action, but a state of being. They connect a noun or an adjective to the subject of a clause or sentence.

Jose was happy.

The plan looks good.

Helping Verbs

Helping verbs help the main verb describe action that happened in the past, is happening in the present, or will happen in the future. There are 23 helping verbs.

am	can	had	might	were
are	could	has	must	will
be	did	have	shall	would
been	do	is	should	
being	does	may	was	

A main verb can have up to three helping verbs.

The bus is coming at three o'clock.

Oops! The bus must have gone at 2:55.

We could have gone on the bus if you hadn't forgotten your backpack in your locker.

Infinitive Form

An ***infinitive*** is a main verb usually preceded by the word ***to***. It does the work of both a verb and a noun, and it may be used as an adjective or adverb.

noun

To go often is her goal. *verb*

I like to play the piano.

A desire to study often brings success in school.

adjective

Verb Tenses

The ***tense*** of a verb tells you the time the action takes place or the state of being—past, present, or future. There are six main tenses:

1 Present tense. The present tense means now.

The dog ***has*** fleas.

I ***go*** to school every day.

2 Past tense. The past tense means before now.

The dog ***had*** fleas until he had a flea shampoo.

I ***went*** to school last week.

3 Future tense. The future tense means not yet.

The dog ***will have*** fleas if he sleeps in the barn.

I ***will go*** to school next Monday.

4 Present perfect tense. The present perfect tense means started in the past and continuing up to the present.

The dog ***has had*** fleas for three years.

I ***have gone*** to school on the bus for years.

5 Past perfect tense. The past perfect tense means finished before some other past action.

The dog ***had had*** fleas for two years before he stopped scratching.

I ***had gone*** to fourth grade before I started fifth grade.

6 Future perfect tense. The future perfect tense means action will start and finish in the future.

The vet ***will have given*** all the puppies a flea collar two months after they are born.

I ***will have gone*** to school for three months before we get a break.

Participles

A ***participle*** is a form of a verb that can be used as a verb or as an adjective. There are two kinds of participles—present and past.

Present participles usually end in -ing and follow the helping verbs for to be **(see p. 43)****.**
Jeff is going to be George Washington in the school pageant.
Amy will be playing Martha Washington.
Past participles usually end in -ed or -en, or -d, -t, or -n, and follow the helping verbs have or had.
Rowan had decided to try out for band instead of the pageant.
Marty and Courtney have been chosen for the parts of John and Abigail Adams.

Principal Parts of Verbs

Each verb has four main parts, called ***principal parts***.
The principal parts include:

1. **The infinitive**
   to swim, to run, to throw
2. **The past tense**
   swam, ran, threw
3. **The present participle**
   (to be) swimming, (to be) running, (to be) throwing
4. **The past participle**
   (have/had) swum, (have/has) run, (have/had) thrown

Regular and Irregular Verbs

Regular verbs are verbs that can be changed from the present to the past and past participle simply by adding ***-ed*** or ***-d***.
Now I jump. Yesterday I jumped. I have jumped.
Now we skate. Yesterday we skated. I have skated.
The past tense and past participles of irregular verbs are formed in unpredictable ways.
You do what you like. I did my homework, and Ian has done his.

To Be or Not to Be

The verb ***to be*** is the most often used verb in the English language. It is an irregular verb. In fact, there are eight different words in the verb to be.
is, am, are, was, were, be, being, been
Now I am. Yesterday I was.
I have been.
Now we are. Yesterday we were. We have been.
Just being here is great!

Chapter 4 Adjectives

Adjectives are words that describe nouns and pronouns. Adjectives ***modify***, or tell more about, nouns. They answer one of three questions:

What kind?
Eric watched the magnificent eagle soar through the sky.

How many?
Katie checked out eight books from the library.

Which one(s)?
Ben took that route to the farm.

Common Adjectives

Common adjectives describe nouns in a general way. These adjectives tell just about anything, from size, shape, and number to color, design, and character.

big, friendly, green, round, spotted, nine
The big dog growled at me.
The friendly dog doesn't growl.
Nine dogs can make a lot of noise.

Proper Adjectives

Proper adjectives are formed from proper nouns. They are always capitalized.

America/American, Asia/Asian, Queen Victoria/Victorian
I love American music.
We have Asian students from China, Japan, and Thailand.
That Victorian house looks haunted.

Demonstrative Adjectives

Demonstrative adjectives are the same words as demonstrative pronouns (see p. 42). As adjectives, they go with nouns and answer the question "Which one(s)?".

that, these, this, those
That movie was great, but those songs were awful.
This candy tastes good, but these peanuts are rotten.

Using Adjectives to Compare

Comparisons can be made on three levels, or ***degrees***—positive, comparative, and superlative.

1 The positive degree describes one thing.

Kyle was ***good*** at solving riddles.

Kyle is ***short***.

2 The comparative degree compares two things.

Kyle's sister was ***better*** than he.

Kyle's sister is ***shorter***.

3 The superlative degree compares three or more things.

Kyle's brother was the ***best*** riddle solver of all.

Kyle's brother is ***shortest***.

To compare adjectives (and adverbs, see p. 48):

1 Add -er and -est to most adjectives that are one or two syllables long.

big/bigger/biggest strong/stronger/strongest

2 If the one- or two-syllable adjective ends in y, drop the y and add -ier and -iest.

happy/happier/happiest homely/homelier/homeliest silly/sillier/silliest

3 Use more and most or less and least in front of most adjectives with two or more syllables.

advanced/more advanced/most advanced capable/more capable/most capable

4 Add -r and -st to short adjectives that end in e.

little/littler/littlest subtle/subtler/subtlest able/abler/ablest

5 Some adjectives are irregular and don't follow these rules, for example:

bad/worse/worst good/better/best

Chapter 5 Adverbs

Adverbs describe verbs, adjectives, or other adverbs. Adverbs are used to make meanings clearer or more exact.

Adverbs and Verbs

Adverbs answer four questions about the verbs they describe — how, when, where, and to what extent?

The young girl jumped high. She danced beautifully.
The tall boy came late. He apologized immediately.
The dog barked loudly when he was here. The child sat there.
The elderly man swam daily. He enjoyed it thoroughly.

Adverbs and Adjectives

Adverbs usually answer the question "How?" when they describe adjectives.

The very young girl danced beautifully.
The extremely tall boy came late.
The annoyingly noisy dog barked loudly.
The exceptionally elderly man swam daily.

Adverbs and Adverbs

Adverbs answer the questions "How?" or "How much?" when they describe other adverbs.

The young girl jumped exceptionally high.
The tall boy came very late.
The noisy dog barked really loudly.
The elderly man swam amazingly fast.

Comparing Adverbs

Adverbs can be compared, just like adjectives, by using the positive, comparative, and superlative degrees (see p. 47).

I run fast enough to make the track team, but Amy runs faster, and Tamika runs fastest.

A Whole New Word:
Making Adverbs from Adjectives

Many adjectives can be changed into adverbs by adding ***-ly*** to the end.

loud/loudly, quick/quickly, bad/badly

But this magic doesn't apply to the three most common adverbs in the English language: ***not***, ***very***, and ***too***.

Chapter 6

Prepositions

A ***preposition*** relates a noun or pronoun to another word in the same sentence. A preposition can also connect a pronoun to a noun in a sentence. A preposition usually tells where something is, where something is going, or when something is happening. A preposition always introduces a phrase. The noun at the end of the prepositional phrase is the ***object of the preposition*** (see also p. 54).

The cups are over the sink.
Lee went to the concert with Kim.
Mary ran to her mother.
The cat ran after the mouse.

List of Common One-, Two-, and Three-Word Prepositions

about
above
according to
across
after
against
ahead of
along
along with
among
around
as
as for
as to
at
away from
because of
before
behind
below
beside
between
beyond
but
by
despite
down
due to
during
except
except for
for
from
in
in addition to
in back of
in case of
in front of
in regard to
inside
in spite of
instead of
into
like
near
of
off
on
on account of
onto
out
out of
outside
over
past
since
through
throughout
to
toward
under
underneath
until
up
upon
up to
with
within
without

(See also Prepositional Phrases, p. 54.)

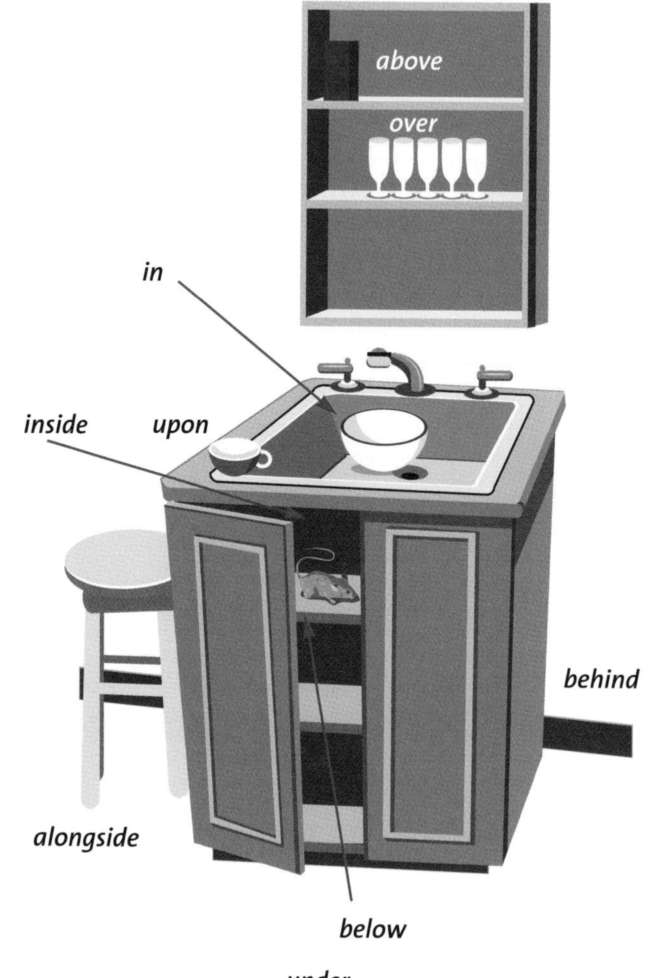

Chapter 7 Conjunctions

Conjunctions are words that join words, phrases, clauses, and sentences.

Coordinating Conjunctions

Coordinating conjunctions join words, phrases, and sentences.

and, but, nor, so, or, yet

The kids came late and baked a cake.
I went to the ballpark but the game was canceled.
I have a sled yet it never snows here.
I can neither eat nor drink before I play soccer.

Subordinating Conjunctions

Subordinating conjunctions join dependent clauses to independent clauses.

after, although, as, as if, because, before, for, if, once, since, so, so that, than, that, though, till, unless, until, when, whenever, where, whereas, wherever, whether, while

Father came home after the work was done.
We were happy once the ice cream was served.
Daniel practiced his music so that he could try out for band.
I cannot go until she comes.

Correlative Conjunctions

Correlative conjunctions are always used in pairs in a phrase or sentence even though they are split up by other words.

both/and, either/or, neither/nor, not only/but also, whether/or

The hungry elephant ate not only the pretzels but also the peanuts.

You should have given him either the pretzels or the peanuts.

Yes, but he wanted to have both the pretzels and the peanuts.

Adverbial Conjunctions

Adverbial conjunctions join clauses or sentences of equal importance.

accordingly, besides, consequently, furthermore, hence, however, likewise, moreover, nevertheless, so, still, therefore, thus

The pretzel bag was left open; consequently, the pretzels went stale.

My dog doesn't like peanuts; however, he loves peanut butter!

I think, therefore I am.

Chapter 8

Interjections

Interjections are words, phrases, and nonsense words that express strong feelings. Interjections are ***interjected*** into, or interrupt, a smooth flow of thoughts to emphasize certain feelings, for example, excitement, happiness, sadness, fear, or anger. Interjections stand apart from sentences and are usually punctuated with exclamation points (see p. 62).

aha, ahem, alas, all right, eureka, gracious, hello, help, hey, oh, oops, ouch, phew, thanks, ugh, well, wow, yikes, yippee, yuck

Aha! **I've caught you!**

Oops! **You put the coin in the wrong slot.**

Yuck! **What a mess!**

Chapter 9

Phrases, Clauses, and Sentences

Some words convey powerful emotion or action just by themselves. But most words need to be combined with other words to get your message across.

Phrases

Phrases are any groups of two or more words that together form a thought or express one meaning. A phrase has no subject or verb. There are four basic types of phrases: prepositional, participial, infinitive and gerund, and verb phrases.

PREPOSITIONAL PHRASES

Prepositional phrases are groups of two or more words that begin with a preposition and end with a noun or pronoun. The noun or pronoun is known as the ***object of the preposition***.

after **the hour**

around **the world**

throughout **the day**

to **them**

object of the preposition

A pronoun immediately following a preposition is always the object of the preposition.

after **her**
by **us**
without **them**

PARTICIPIAL PHRASES

Participial phrases are groups of two or more words that begin with ***participles*** (see p. 45).

writing **a book**
grasping **his sword**
leaping **to my feet**

INFINITIVE AND GERUND PHRASES

Infinitive phrases are groups of two or more words consisting of an infinitive verb or an infinitive verb plus an adverb. Infinitive verbs are easily identified. They begin with the word ***to***.

to go
to go boldly
to play
to care deeply

Gerund phrases are groups of two or more words that contain a gerund. A gerund is a verb form that ends in ***-ing*** and acts as a noun.

my being there
his going to the moon
your wanting a new skateboard

Appositives

Appositives follow the nouns, pronouns, or phrases in clauses that they describe. Appositives can be one word or a whole phrase. Appositives are separated from a main clause or sentence with commas.

Boston, Massachusetts, is north of Providence, Rhode Island.

Freddy, Sue Ellen's dog, howled.

VERB PHRASES

Verb phrases are groups of two or more verbs that describe an action. They are made up of a main verb and one or more helping verbs.

have come
had gone
will be coming
would have come
should be going

(See also Participles, p. 45.)

Clauses

Clauses are groups of two or more words that have a ***subject*** and a ***predicate***. Clauses are either ***principal*** or ***subordinate***.

PRINCIPAL CLAUSES

Principal clauses are also called ***independent***, or ***main***, ***clauses***. Only principal clauses can stand alone as complete ***sentences*** (see pp. 57–59).

The dog was sick.

The dog ate grass, and the cat licked her paws.

SUBORDINATE CLAUSES

Subordinate clauses are also called ***dependent clauses***. Subordinate clauses express ideas or information related to principal clauses.

The dog was sick because he ate grass.

The cat licked her paws after she played with the yarn.

> **Subordinate clauses cannot stand alone as sentences. They are combined with principal clauses to complete thoughts or give greater meaning to a sentence.**

Subjects and Predicates:
Simple, Complete, and Compound

A ***simple subject*** is the noun or pronoun that tells who or what a clause or sentence is about.

The boy played soccer.

A ***complete subject*** is the noun plus any descriptive word or phrase that goes with it.

The athletic boy on the football field played soccer.

A ***compound subject*** is two or more simple subjects joined by a conjunction (see p. 51).

My mother and I watched the boy play soccer.

A ***simple predicate*** is just the verb in the predicate.

The horse whinnied.

A ***complete predicate*** is the verb plus any descriptive words or phrases that make up the predicate. It is everything in a clause or sentence that is not contained in the complete subject.

The horse whinnied loudly at the trainer.

A ***compound predicate*** is found in sentences where two or more different actions are described.

The horse whinnied and snorted.

Sentences

Sentences are groups of words that express a complete thought. You can make a sentence by putting together a noun (subject) and a verb (predicate).

Sentences can be short or long, simple or complicated. But all sentences fall into one of three categories: simple, compound, or complex.

Noun (subject)	Verb (predicate)
I	go.
He	runs.
Mosquitoes	bite.
People	care.

SIMPLE SENTENCES

A ***simple sentence*** is made up of one **subject** and one predicate.

The boys played baseball.
The boys played baseball against the girls' team.
The boys from Middletown played against the Hightown girls' team.

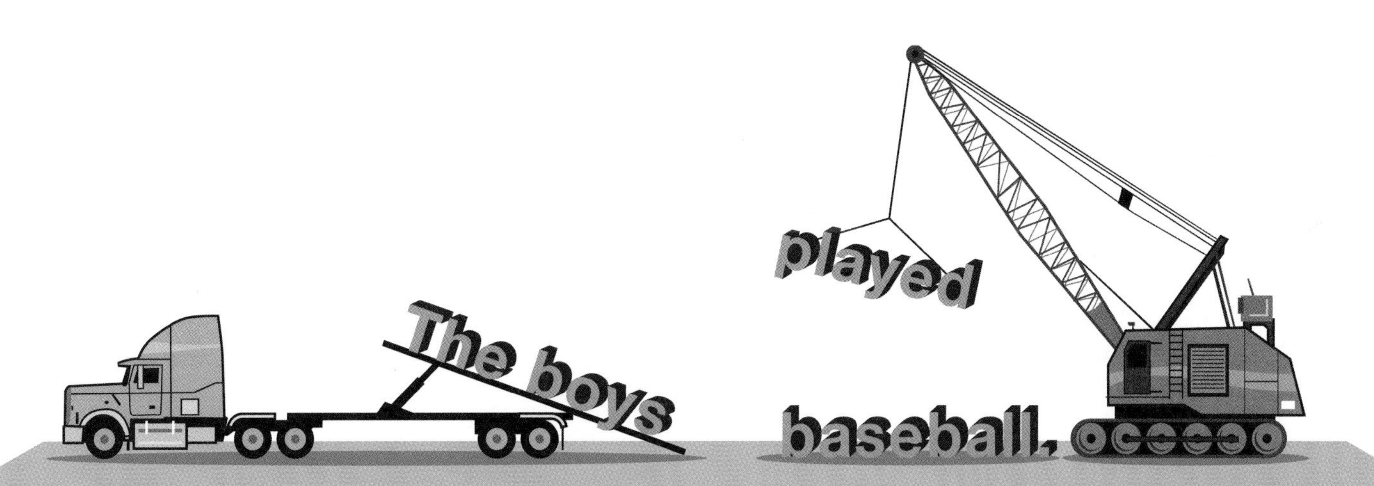

COMPOUND SENTENCES

A ***compound sentence*** is made up of two or more simple sentences joined by a conjunction (see pp. 51–52).

The girls played baseball and they beat the other team.

I go to the playground with my brother every day, but yesterday he wouldn't play with me.

I like broccoli raw yet I can't eat it cooked.

COMPLEX SENTENCES

A ***complex sentence*** is made up of a principal clause and one or more subordinate clauses.

Fighting infection was difficult until penicillin was discovered.

When I forgot my lunch, I had to eat that gross cafeteria food.

The fifth graders left the playground early because it started to rain.

Four Types of Sentences

DECLARATIVE SENTENCES

Declarative sentences make statements.

Life is good.
I am happy, and you are sad.
You ate an extra scoop of ice cream.

INTERROGATIVE SENTENCES

Interrogative sentences ask questions.

Is life good?
Are you happy, too?
Did your stomach hurt after you ate the fifth scoop of ice cream?

IMPERATIVE SENTENCES

Imperative sentences give commands or request action.

Go.
Open the door, and go inside.
After you open the door, go inside.

EXCLAMATORY SENTENCES

Exclamatory sentences express strong feelings or emotions. They end in exclamation points (see p. 62) instead of periods.

I feel horrible!
I ate a whole pizza and I'm still hungry!
I studied hard, so I got the highest score on the test!

You Understood

Imperative sentences often don't have subjects—or do they? When you give a command, you are addressing someone else. He or she knows whom you're talking to. The ***you*** is the subject, and whether or not you say it, ***you*** is understood.

(You) **Leave my cat alone.**
(You) **Go.**

PUNCTUATION MARKS
and Some of Their Uses

Apostrophe (')

1. Shows possession

Jamai's shoe, the girls' toys, Mary's and John's boats

2. Shows contractions

can't, she's, would've, '98

3. Creates plurals of lowercase letters

a's, b's, c's

Colon (:)

1. Introduces lists

The clock has three parts: a face, a dial, and numbers.

2. Introduces excerpts and long quotations

As Lincoln wrote in his Gettysburg Address:

> "Fourscore and seven years ago, our fathers brought forth on this continent a new nation, conceived in liberty, and dedicated to the proposition that all men are created equal."

3. Separates hours from minutes when writing time in numerals

2:00, 4:15, 8:55

4. Punctuates the greeting in a formal letter

Dear Ms. President:

Comma (,)

1. Separates clauses in sentences, including long compound sentences

The rain came, which was very good for the crops.

2. Separates items in a series

I want a baseball, a glove, and a bat for my birthday.

3. Separates three or more adjectives in a series

I saw red, green, yellow, and orange kites.

4. Separates a direct quotation in a sentence

Marty said, "Get out of there!"

5. **Separates a city from a state**
   Minneapolis, Minnesota
6. **Separates the month and day from the year in a date**
   June 6, 2005
7. **Sets apart mild interjections from the rest of a sentence**
   Gosh, I was hungry.
8. **Sets apart appositives**
   Bill, my brother, was late.
9. **Punctuates the greeting and closing in a friendly letter**
   Dear Sally,
   Your friend,

Dash (—)

1. **Works like a comma to separate phrases or clauses in a sentence**
   President Clinton — along with many others — studied law before entering politics.
2. **Works like a colon to separate lists**
   I had three choices — stand, run, or sit.
3. **Works like an ellipsis to show interrupted or unfinished statements**
   I would never have guessed, but then —
4. **Works like a comma to separate appositives**
   My father — a great guy — built a boxcar for the derby.

Ellipsis (. . .)

1. **Replaces words left out in the middle of a quote or obvious text**
   I pledge allegiance to . . . America.
2. **Shows that a thought or list should continue in the same pattern**
   A is for apple, b is for box, c is for cow . . .

3. **A period followed by three ellipsis points shows that words have been left out at the end of a sentence, paragraph, or longer piece of writing.**
   I pledge allegiance to the flag. . . .

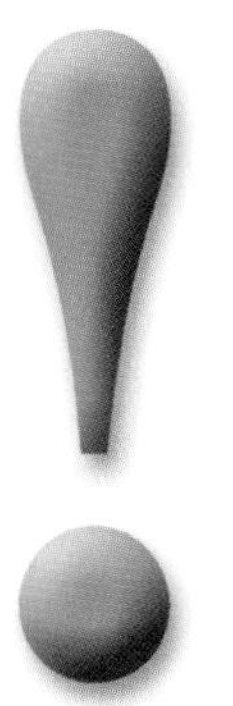

Exclamation point (!)

1. Ends exclamatory sentences

I won!

2. Separates an interjection from a sentence

Hooray! I won!

3. Ends strong imperative sentences

Get away from the fire!

Hyphen (-)

1. Connects two-part words

roly-poly, twenty-two, air-conditioning

2. Separates words into syllables

ap-ple

3. Connects compound nouns and adjectives

well-known man, teacher-in-training

4. Separates some prefixes

ex-champion, re-create

5. Divides words at the end of a line of writing

diction-
ary

nota-
tion

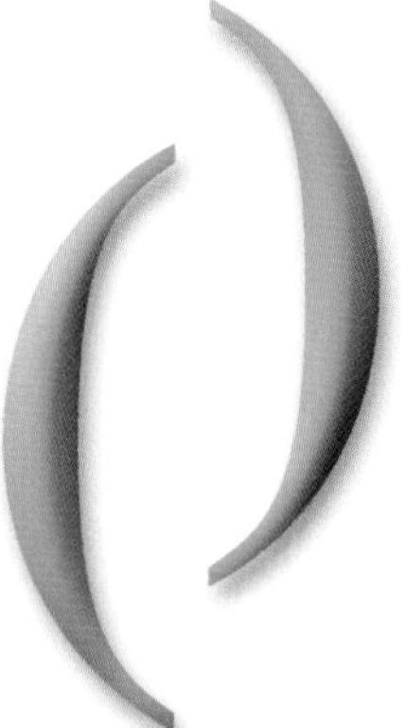

Parentheses ( )

1. Hold additional information in a sentence, but information that is not necessary to include in the sentence

I'll tell you (and you can listen to) my story.

The girl was born (two weeks early) in Florida.

2. Hold explanatory information or alternative spellings, names, or symbols

The gorgon (a mythical monster) frightened the sailors.

The price was stated as fifteen dollars ($15).

Period (.)

1. Ends a declarative sentence

I will go to the zoo today.

2. Follows most initials

John F. Kennedy was a popular president.

3. Follows most abbreviations

The giraffe was 12 ft. tall.

4. Follows numerals when writing lists

1. Trading Cards
2. Bubble Gum, etc.
3. Milk

Question mark (?)

1. Ends an interrogative sentence

What are you doing up there?

2. Shows doubt or uncertainty when written in parentheses

King Tut lived 3,000 (?) years ago.

Quotation marks (“ ”)

1. Show a person’s exact words

The teacher said, “Start writing.”

2. Set apart titles of articles in magazines and newspapers

Did you read the story “Amazing Facts” in Sunday’s paper?

3. Set apart chapter titles in books as well as essay, short story, song, and poem titles

“Getting Started” is the title of the first chapter of *Building a Treehouse*.

4. Set apart special words and phrases, including slang, nonstandard English, and technical words

The answer to the clue “fruity” was the word “apple.”

5. When single (‘/’), show a quotation within another quotation

“The teacher said, ‘You kids are too much,’ when we locked the classroom door,” Fred explained to the principal.

Semicolon (;)

1. Joins related independent clauses into one sentence when they are not joined by a conjunction

The Great Houdini died; he could not make his greatest escape.

2. Sets apart items in a list, particularly items following a colon

This is what we need to do for the party: send the invitations; bake the cake; buy the candles, paper plates, napkins, and forks; and reserve the party room.

Underline (____)

1. Sets apart book, movie, play, opera, TV show, and video titles

Have you read Little House on the Prairie?

2. Sets apart the names of newspapers and magazines

I read the article in Junior Scholastic.

3. Sets apart foreign words and phrases

Adiós, my good friends.

4. Adds emphasis to words and phrases

She told us never to eat with our hands.

He mentioned a long time ago that he would be going.

Note: In typeset books or on a word processor, italic type (or *italics*) is used in place of underlining. Italic type looks a little like cursive handwriting. In this book's typeface, *italic type looks like this.*

Sentence Diagrams

Sentence diagrams illustrate how parts of speech work to form complete thoughts or ***sentences*** (see also p. 57). Sentence diagrams also show the main parts of a sentence and the words and phrases that are added to communicate greater detail or more precise information.

Life is good.

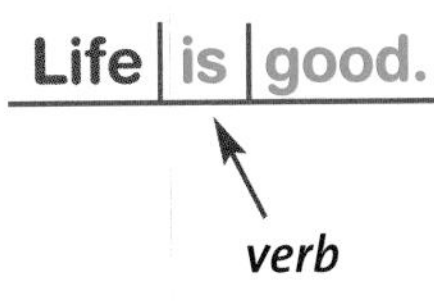

You ate an extra scoop of ice cream.

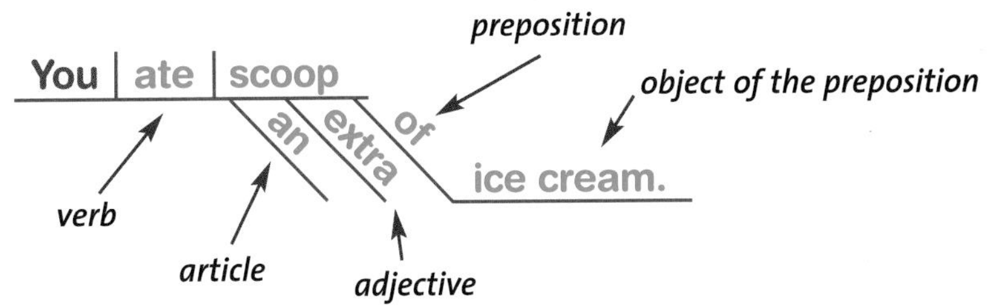

Open the door.

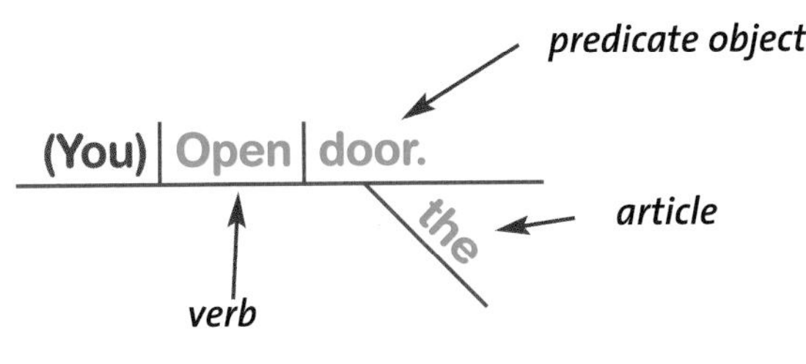

I am opening the door.

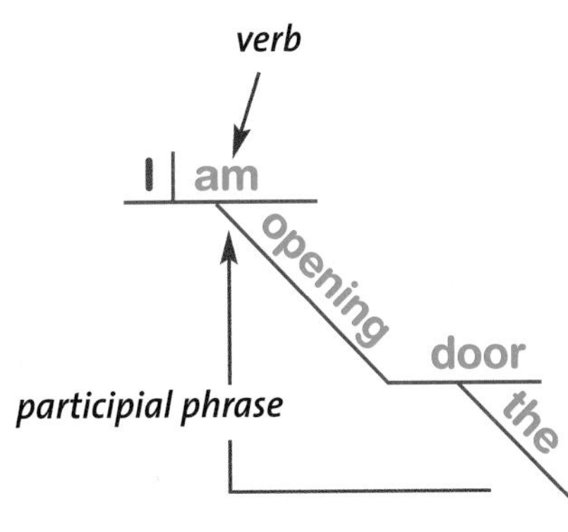

Yes, the hungry elephant ate not only pretzels but also peanuts.

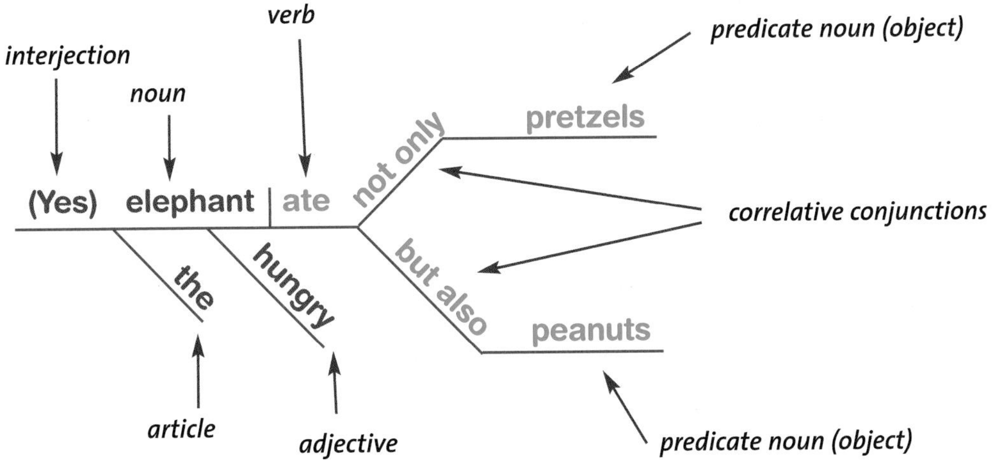

■ Subject ■ Predicate

Chapter 10 Combining Sentences to Make Paragraphs

Paragraphs are groups of sentences that describe related ideas. A good paragraph includes the following: a topic sentence, detail sentences, proper order, and a consistent theme. In practical writing (see pp. 98–111), the sentences within a paragraph combine to develop the ideas and point of view of the writing. In creative writing (see pp. 88–97), sentences combine into paragraphs to flesh out essential details of the story, such as character description, setting, dialogue, and theme (see also p. 93).

Topic Sentences

The ***topic sentence*** states the theme or main idea of a paragraph. It is usually the first sentence of a paragraph, but it can also be found at the end. A topic sentence is almost never found in the middle of a paragraph.

Detail Sentences

Detail sentences tell more about the main idea of the paragraph.

Order of Sentences

The ***order of sentences*** is important in writing good paragraphs. For example, if you wrote a paragraph explaining the four steps in flossing your teeth, you wouldn't start by writing, "Throw away the used dental floss." Order should always make sense.

Theme

The ***theme***, or main idea, holds together all the sentences in a paragraph. It is stated in the topic sentence. Be sure all the detail sentences stick to the theme and tell about the main idea. Sentences that do not belong upset the sense or flow in the order of the sentences. The sentences that don't make sense are called ***non sequiturs***, or ideas that "don't follow."

Different Paragraphs for Different Purposes: Chronological, Cause and Effect, and Compare and Contrast

Paragraphs can be constructed for different purposes. When they are used to describe sequences and time frames, they are ***chronological paragraphs***. Some paragraphs describe events and what happens after they occur. These paragraphs describe ***cause and effect***. Still other paragraphs are organized to point out similarities and differences in two or more things. These paragraphs ***compare and contrast***.

Writing in chronological, cause and effect, and compare and contrast forms isn't simply used to organize sentences within paragraphs, however. These forms are also used to organize essays and other longer pieces of practical writing (see p. 98).

Topic Sentence. Remember, the topic sentence states the theme of the paragraph. It is usually the first sentence.

Growing orange plants is as easy as one-two-three. First save the seeds from the next orange you eat. Next, place the seeds about one inch apart on top of a container filled with potting soil. Last, cover with about a quarter inch of additional potting soil, water, and wait. If you keep your container in a sunny place and make sure the soil stays moist, your orange seeds should sprout in two to three weeks.

Detail Sentences. In this paragraph, the writer tells more about growing orange plants.

Order of Sentences. In order to make sense, the detail sentences must follow a logical order or sequence. Imagine rewriting the paragraph starting with the third sentence. It would make no sense.

Writing Tools

Chapter 1 Outlines and Story Maps

Outlines: Skeletons for Organized Writers

Outlines are tools that are used in the planning stages of writing, sometimes called ***prewriting***. Outlines help you organize ideas for a school report or a speech. If you have a hard time getting all your ideas into an outline, it may mean you have chosen too large a topic. For example, it you are reporting on a trip to the zoo, you might find it easier to write about one of the exhibits or one zoo activity rather than try to describe every exhibit that you visited or every animal that you saw. A story on big cats or feeding time will allow you to say a lot on one interesting subject.

Outlines include three basic elements: a title, main headings, and subheadings. Together these elements help you create logical beginnings, middles, and endings for your work. Outlines also help you decide where it makes sense to include the information you want.

Bats

I. The Body
A. Wings
1. Only mammal that can fly
a. They fly more slowly than most birds
b. They can fly through tiny gaps and holes

TITLE
*The **title** should tell the subject of the work. The title of the outline may or may not become the title of the paper.*

2. The wings contract and fold along the bones when bats aren't flying

B. Head and Body

1. Strange face, sometimes really scary or ugly looking
2. Huge ears
3. Legs, but no arms-only wings
4. Sleep upside down

C. Senses

1. Almost blind
2. Echolocation
    a. Produce high-pitched sound
    b. Sound works like radar to help bat locate food or obstacles

II. Eating Habits

A. Most eat insects

B. Mice or other bats

C. Flower nectar

D. Fruit

III. Life Cycle and Habitat

A. Live up to 20 years

B. Live birth, usually one baby at a time

C. Live almost anywhere in the world

1. Not in extremely cold places
2. Not on some islands

D. Some species migrate to find food

E. Species in cold climates hibernate in winter

MAIN HEADINGS
Main headings *state the main topics covered in the paper. The first is the opening paragraph, and the last is the conclusion. You can include as few as two other main headings or as many as you need to cover your subject. To show main headings, use a capital Roman numeral and a period.*

SUBHEADINGS
Subheadings *come under main headings. For the first level of subheadings, use capital letters. For the second level of subheadings, use Arabic numerals.*

Story Maps: The Path of Fiction

Story maps or ***plans*** are outlines for fiction writers. You can "map" the main parts of stories or plays: setting, characters, major events, problems (challenges), and solutions.

Story maps can be laid out in many different ways. Unlike outlines, you don't have to give the map a title or use Roman numerals. But, to be useful, the maps should include all the main parts of the story or play. These main parts should be organized around a ***plot*** (see p. 81), or action line.

Story Map

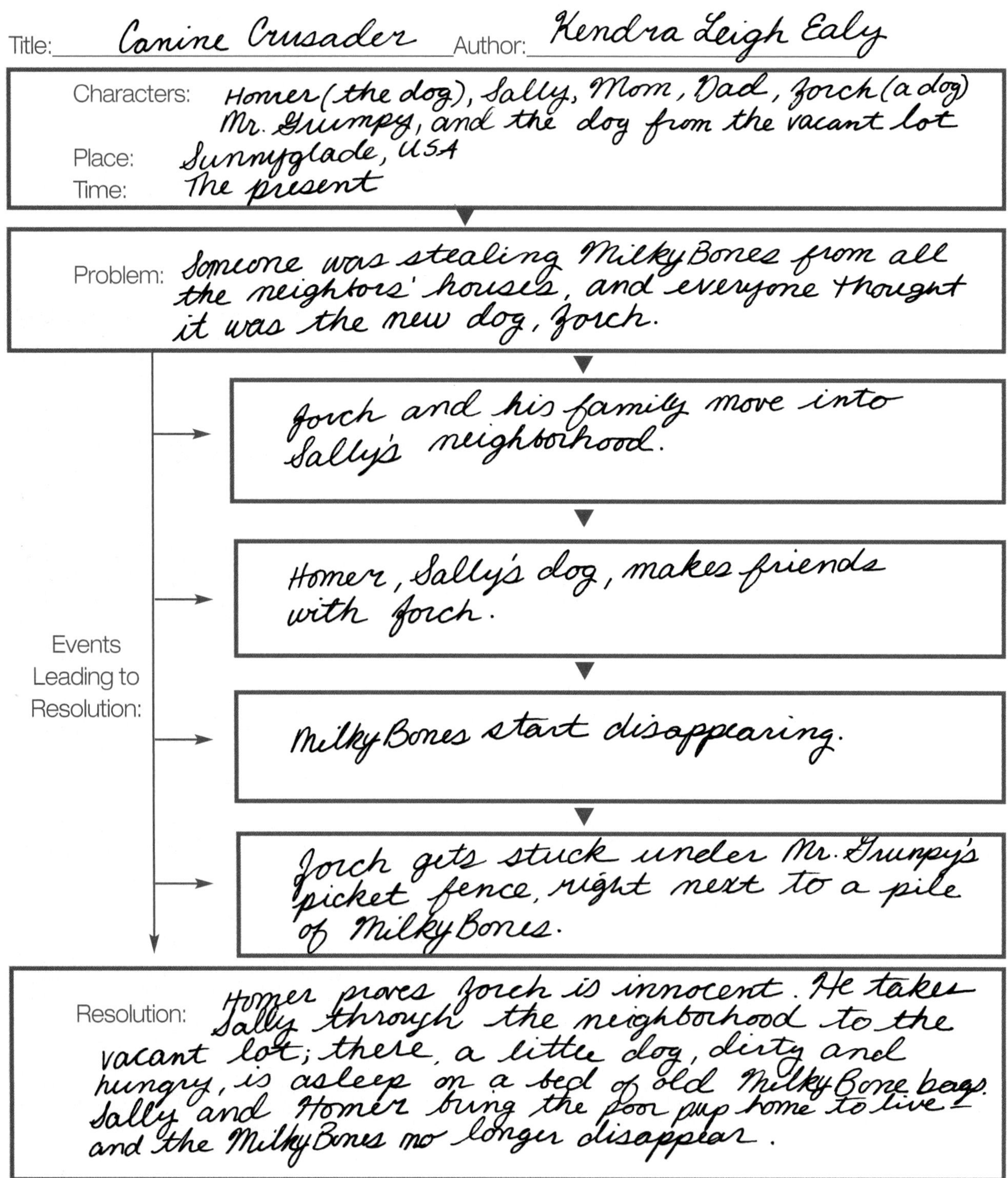

Title: Canine Crusader Author: Kendra Leigh Ealy

Characters: Homer (the dog), Sally, Mom, Dad, Jorch (a dog) Mr. Grumpy, and the dog from the vacant lot

Place: Sunnyglade, USA

Time: The present

Problem: Someone was stealing MilkyBones from all the neighbors' houses, and everyone thought it was the new dog, Jorch.

Events Leading to Resolution:

- Jorch and his family move into Sally's neighborhood.
- Homer, Sally's dog, makes friends with Jorch.
- MilkyBones start disappearing.
- Jorch gets stuck under Mr. Grumpy's picket fence, right next to a pile of MilkyBones.

Resolution: Homer proves Jorch is innocent. He takes Sally through the neighborhood to the vacant lot; there, a little dog, dirty and hungry, is asleep on a bed of old MilkyBone bags. Sally and Homer bring the poor pup home to live — and the MilkyBones no longer disappear.

Circle Story Framework

Use a ***circle story framework*** to establish ***sequence***, or the order of events in your story.

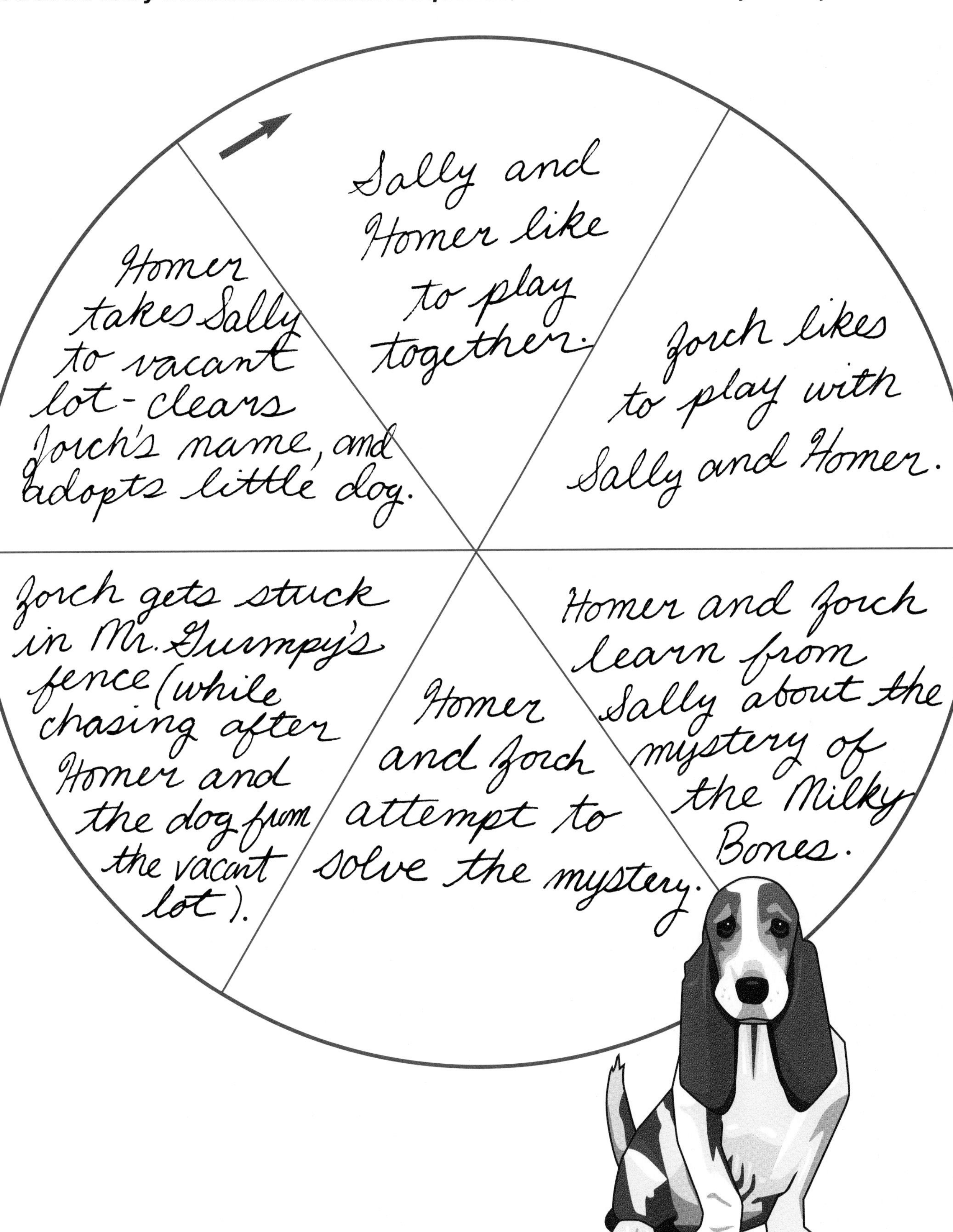

Flow Chart

A ***flow chart*** and a ***time line*** can be used much the same way as a ***circle story framework***.

Sally and Homer like to play together.

↓

Zorch likes to play with Sally and Homer.

↓

Homer and Zorch learn from Sally about the mystery of the Milky Bones.

→

Homer and Zorch attempt to solve the mystery.

↓

Zorch gets stuck in Mr. Grumpy's fence (while chasing Homer).

↓

Homer takes Sally to vacant lot, clears Zorch's name, and adopts little dog.

Time Line

1a	Sally and Homer like to play together.
1b	Zorch likes to play with Sally and Homer.
2	Homer and Zorch learn from Sally about the mystery of the Milky Bones.
3	Homer and Zorch attempt to solve the mystery.
4	Zorch gets stuck in Mr. Grumpy's fence (while chasing after Homer and the dog from the vacant lot).
5	Homer takes Sally to vacant lot - clears Zorch's name, and adopts little dog.

Cause/Effect Diagram

Cause: Milky Bones are stolen.

Effect: Neighbors are upset-want to find thief.

Effect: Sally tells Homer and Zorch.

Effect: Homer and Zorch attempt to solve crime.

Cause: Neighbor's Milky Bones are missing.

Cause: Zorch is new dog in town.

Cause: Milky Bones found near hole in vacant lot.

Effect: Zorch is blamed for stealing Milky Bones.

Venn Diagram

Use ***Venn diagrams*** to compare two or more characters or events.

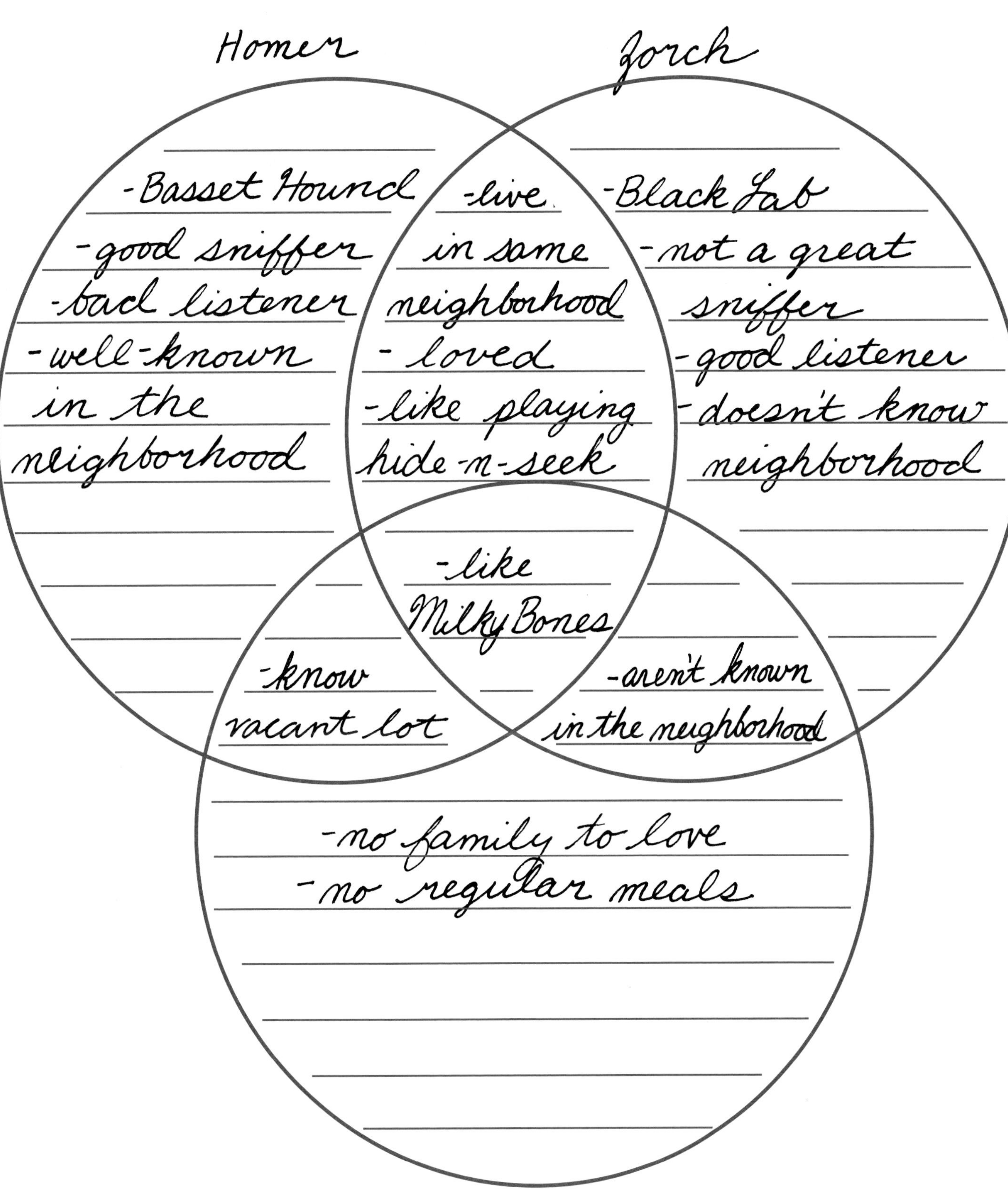

Chapter 2 Rough Draft to Final Copy

Once you've prepared an ***outline*** or a ***story map***, you're ready to write the ***rough*** or ***first draft***. The rough draft is also called ***sloppy copy***.

Rough drafts help you organize your ideas into sentences. They also help show how the different parts of your writing fit together. The rough draft can be written in pen or pencil on paper, or the draft can be keyboarded using word processing software on a computer. No matter how you choose to make your rough draft, it's a good idea to skip a line or double space your work. This will give you room to make corrections on pen-and-paper and printed computer drafts, and will also make reading on the computer monitor easier.

The rough draft is ***not*** the final copy. You may write several drafts before the final one. Don't worry about style and catchy phrases at this point. Instead, follow these basic steps:

1. Read over your outline, notes, or story map.
2. Follow your outline or map to write down in sentences the main points of the story.
3. Write down all your thoughts without stopping to check spelling or grammar, or to edit. Put in as much appropriate information as you can.
4. Read over your rough draft for obvious mistakes. Change sentences and paragraphs that do not follow logically. Mark corrections in grammar and punctuation (see next page).
5. Read over the rough draft for style. Consider how you might use some basic tools and techniques (see Terms and Techniques in Writing, pp. 78–82) to add drama or interest to your writing. Fill in details in your paper, or add minor characters, dialogue, or extra episodes to your fiction.
6. Put the rough draft aside for a while and then read it over again. Is there anything you want to rewrite? Would you like to show it to a friend or family member? Have you made your points clear? Try reading your work aloud to see if it sounds right. Fine-tune your copy.
7. Prepare a final draft.

Skip a space between lines when you write your rough draft. Then you'll have plenty of room to make corrections or additions later.

Every Author Needs an Editor

Editing Sense and Symbols

Every author needs to go over the drafts of his or her writing and edit for sense, flow, and simple errors in grammar and spelling. Following are examples of basic editing symbols and a draft of a paragraph edited to create an improved piece of writing.

~~To grow an~~ orange place is ~~simple.~~ First save the sedes from oranges you eat. ~~Second,~~ ~~put~~ the seeds ~~in soil in a pot~~ and cover with soil. ~~then water the soil.~~ Keep the pot in the sun and keep watering. According to my mother, You should have oranges in two to tree weeks"

symbol	meaning	example
ℯ	delete	I went to the park ~~on Monday.~~
^	left out, insert	I went to the park^. (yesterday)
∿	reverse order of letters (transpose)	I went to the park yetserday.
⁀	close up, no space	I went to the park ~~on Monday.~~
≡	write in capitals	I went to the park on monday.
. . .	stet (let it stand)	I went to the park ~~on Monday.~~
¶	start new paragraph	I went to the park on Monday. Everyone was there, except Mary. She was home with the mumps. ¶ Eric brought a soccer ball.
⊙	insert period	I went to the park⊙ I played on the swings.
^,	insert comma	I went to the park, ate candy, and played.
˅"	insert quotation marks	I said, "Wait for me!"
˅'	insert apostrophe	The park's benches are green.

Chapter 3

Terms and Techniques in Writing

Alliteration

Repetition of the same sound at the beginning of two or more words that are next to each other or near each other.

Fly away, my fine-feathered friend.

Drat! I'd deem that a dastardly deed, Duane!

A silvery sliver slid from the needle case.

Allusion

Something or someone talked about through hints. ***Allusions*** are often made to people, places, and things that are already well known.

The poor dog died this afternoon. Now he is off to the big kennel in the sky. (Big kennel in the sky is heaven.)

He's no George Washington. (George Washington means honest person.)

Assonance

Vowel rhyme, or words that have the same vowel sound. ***Assonance*** is often used in poetry.

The slowly growing mighty oak did shade our home for years.

Cacophony

Noise, or harsh, unpleasant combinations of sounds. ***Cacophony*** is used in poetry for special effects. It is created by reading onomatopoeic words (see p. 81), or by adding sounds based on the author's instructions, for example, clapping hands, whistling, striking a triangle, etc.

Characters

The personalities in a story. Most ***characters*** are people, but sometimes characters are pets, wild animals, or fantasy creatures. The most important character in a book, story, play, or poem is called the ***main character***. Other characters are called ***secondary***, or ***supporting***, ***characters***.

In true stories, characters are drawn from real life. The main character in a biography is the person about whom the story is written. The secondary characters are people who have known or have somehow been involved with the life of the main character.

In fictional stories, characters are often good or bad, friendly or mean.

The "good" main character is called the ***protagonist*** and the "bad" main character is called the ***antagonist***. A story can have many antagonists, but usually only one protagonist.

Many fictional characters suffer from a weakness called a ***character flaw***. This flaw is important to the action or plot of the story (see Achilles' heel, p. 115) because it is the reason the character gets in trouble or falls into danger.

Climax

The high point of a story. It is followed by an ending called a ***resolution***, or ***denouement***.

Composition

Any written work, either fiction or nonfiction.

Dialogue

Conversation or talking that takes place between two or more characters. Dialogue is usually enclosed in quotation marks.

Figure of Speech

A word or phrase used to describe something in an imaginative and usually unrelated way. (See also ***allusion***, ***imagery***, ***metaphor***, and ***simile***.)

Hyperbole

A deliberate exaggeration used as a figure of speech.

My dog is as big as a ten-ton elephant!

Their house was so big, you had to drive a car from the front door to the living room.

Imagery

Word painting, or creating imaginary pictures with words. ***Imagery*** helps readers form pictures in their minds. These pictures make certain points easier to understand and more interesting to read. Such techniques as ***allusion***, ***metaphor***, and ***simile*** are examples of imagery.

My dog is very happy. (without imagery)
My dog is a pig in mud. (allusion)
The boy would not sit down at his desk. (without imagery)
The boy's desk might as well have been made of pins and needles. (metaphor)
The yellow house was located on the top of a grassy hill. (without imagery)
The house seemed to bloom atop the hill like a daffodil in April. (simile)

The house bloomed atop the hill.

Metaphor

A comparison of two different things to show a likeness between them that does not use ***like*** or ***as***.

The teacher chimed the roll call.
Alice was drowning in tears.

Meter

The rhythm made by stressed and unstressed syllables in poetry.

There was a crooked man who walked a crooked mile . . .
There once was a penguin named Dave . . .

Mood

The feeling of a story, short story, poem, or play. Moods can be happy, sad, scary, tense, gloomy, etc.

Nonfiction

A piece of writing that tells about people, places, or events that exist, that are happening, or that have existed or happened in the past. Nonfiction can also express an opinion or a true feeling.

Onomatopoeia

Words that are invented to imitate real sounds. ***Bang***, ***zip***, ***smash***, ***rip***, and ***grrrrrr*** are all examples of onomatopoeia.

Parable

A story with a moral or religious lesson to be learned. Parables are related to fables.

Personification

Attributing to things that are not human the personalities and actions of humans. Through personification, Pooh and Paddington behave like human children, not like bear cubs. Feelings can also be personified; for example, ***fear grabbed*** the victim in its ***icy clutches***.

Plot

The actions or events in a short story, novel, or play.

Poetry

A feeling or story told in rhythmic verse. Poetry sometimes uses ***rhyme*** and ***imagery***. A work of poetry is called a ***poem***. (See also Writing Poetry, p. 88, and Poem Types and Terms, p. 89.)

Prose

Any writing that is like ordinary speech, unlike poetry.

Rhyme

The repetition of similar or identical sounds, for example:

red **green**
bed **bean**

Setting

The time and place in which a story, poem, or play takes place. A setting can be a forest, a house, a city, the present, the past, the future, etc.

Simile

A figure of speech that compares two unlike things. Similes are often confused with ***metaphors***. A major difference between similes and metaphors is that a simile is introduced by the words ***like*** or ***as***, and a metaphor is not.

The lion purred like a kitten.

Kim cried as if it were the end of the world.

Subject

The ***theme***, ***topic***, or ***main idea*** of a sentence, paragraph, or larger piece of writing.

Theme

The ***main idea*** or ***topic*** in a piece of writing.

Tone

The feeling in a piece of writing, similar to mood. ***Tone*** or ***tone of voice*** reflects the feeling of the writer as much as the feeling in the writing. Tone can be nasty, kind, persuasive, angry, friendly, etc.

Topic

The main idea in a piece of writing.

Chapter 4 Understanding Other People's Writing

The tools you use to help you write — outlines and story maps — can also be used to help you understand other people's writing. So, too, can Venn diagrams, circle story frameworks, flow charts, time lines, and cause/effect diagrams.

Look at the following story about bats. It's broken down into outline pieces. Compare the pieces to the outline for this story (see pp. 68–69).

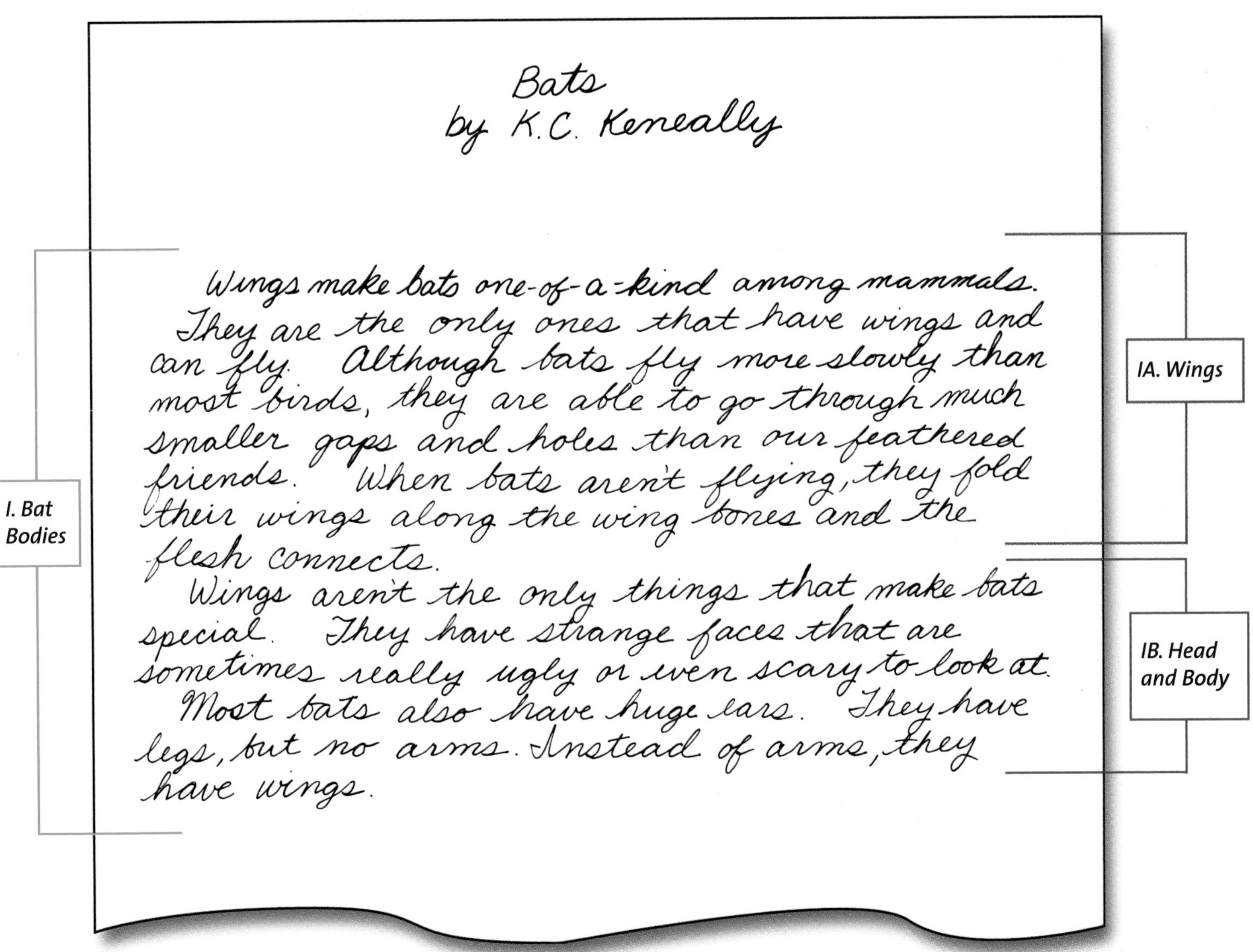

Bats
by K.C. Keneally

Wings make bats one-of-a-kind among mammals. They are the only ones that have wings and can fly. Although bats fly more slowly than most birds, they are able to go through much smaller gaps and holes than our feathered friends. When bats aren't flying, they fold their wings along the wing bones and the flesh connects.

Wings aren't the only things that make bats special. They have strange faces that are sometimes really ugly or even scary to look at. Most bats also have huge ears. They have legs, but no arms. Instead of arms, they have wings.

IC. Senses

Bats are mostly blind. Maybe you've heard the expression "blind as a bat"? Instead of seeing with their eyes, bats use echolocation. They send out a high-pitched sound that bounces off food and obstacles like radar. The bounced back sounds are picked up by receptors near the bat's ears.
Bats also sleep upside down.

II. Eating Habits

Most bats eat insects. Some eat mice or even other bats. Still other bats prefer flower nectar or fruits.

III. Life Cycle and Habitat

Bats can live up to 20 years. They are born live, like other mammals, and usually one at a time.
Except for remote islands and extremely cold places, bats are found everywhere in the world. Some bats survive happily in one place all year round. Others have to migrate to find food. In colder climates, bats hibernate during winter months when food is scarce.

Now look at the short story below. See how it can be broken down into the elements of a story map.

Characters

Place

Canine Crusaders
by Kendra Leigh Ealy

Setting

"Homer, fetch!" Sally Smith called to her dog. She tossed a Milky Bone toward the backyard fence of her home in Sunnyglade.

The bassett hound ran down the porch step and across the lawn. Then he raised his snout, positioned himself, caught the Milky Bone in his mouth, and plopped down on the spot to enjoy the tasty treat. Just then, a furry black streak flew over the fence and across the grass toward Homer.

"Zorch! Zorch, leave Homer alone!" Sally called after the streak. "I've got a treat for you, too!"

Zorch belonged to the Jeffersons. He and his family had just moved in next door. Zorch and Homer made friends on the spot.

Zorch couldn't have had a better friend than Homer. Everyone around Elm Street—everyone except Mr. Grumpy, of course—loved the sweet-tempered bassett and his constant companion, Sally. So everyone kept a bone or two on hand for their favorite dog. Zorch was quick to understand that Homer was top dog on Elm Street and, by association, he'd be popular, too!

Problem

Zorch was hounding Homer less than a week when the mystery of the Milky Bones began. The whole neighborhood was buzzing with the news. No sooner did Sally jump off the school bus than she heard all about it. Everybody's Milky Bones were missing!

Sally ran home, "Mom, where are the bones? Do you know the story? All the dog bones in the neighborhood are gone! Mom, did you hear?"

"Sally, Sally. Calm down," her mother said. "Yes, I've heard the news-but not before our Milky Bones were missing, too."

"Where'd they go, Mom?"

Homer bounded into the kitchen to greet Sally. He was about to leap to her waist and give her a lick, but she didn't open her arms for the greeting. Instead, he cocked his head to listen.

"Well dear, if we knew where the bones were, there wouldn't be a mystery," her mother replied. "The neighbors seem to think Zorch is the culprit, though."

"That's not fair!" Sally cried. "Zorch wouldn't do that!"

Development of problem toward resolution

"Maybe not, dear, but that's what folks are saying," her mother said.

Sally and Homer moped out the back door and into the yard. No sooner had they hit the lawn than a black streak came flying over the fence.

"Not now, Zorch," Sally scolded. "This is no time for games—and no time for bones, either. You didn't steal the bones, did you, boy?"

Zorch sat near Sally's feet and cocked his head quizzically.

"Of course you didn't, Zorch," Sally answered her own question. "But we've gotta solve this mystery and get you off the hook."

Sally and the dogs walked around the house to Elm Street and turned along Spruce. "Am I imagining it," thought Sally, "or are people giving Zorch dirty looks?" The uncertain feeling grew stronger as she walked with the dogs over to Chestnut and around the corner onto Maple.

Just then, Homer picked up a scent. His hound dog instincts kicked in as he pressed his nose to the ground and slowly inched foward, following the trail of some mysterious odor. Homer was picking up speed, fast on the trail of something—on a canine crusade, Sally thought. Sally and Zorch followed Homer to the end of the block toward Mr. Grumpy's.

"Homer! Stay out of old man Grumpy's yard," she called. Mr. Grumpy was the only neighbor who never had a Milky Bone—or a kind word—for Homer.

But Homer followed the scent right into Mr. Grumpy's yard. Then, suddenly, Zorch bolted toward Mr. Grumpy's, too. Before Sally could stop them, the dogs ran out of sight toward mean Mr. Grumpy's backyard.

By the time Sally reached Grumpy's backyard, Homer was nowhere to be seen. Zorch was stuck under the backyard fence and barking his head off, and old man Grumpy was shouting from his back door.

"Get those vermin dogs outta my yard. I'll call the pound, I'm telling ya! Get those mutts outta here now!" Grumpy's threats were likely to become promises, Sally knew. She had to get Zorch unstuck and find Homer.

Sally knelt by Zorch and stroked his back. Zorch turned his head and gazed at her from the other side of the wire fencing. He took a deep breath and relaxed his muscles. Sally thought he would pull himself back into Grumpy's yard, but Zorch eased himself forward instead. He got clear of the fence and tore off behind Grumpy's toward the vacant lot. Sally chased after him and then Sally stopped, panting. She looked across the vacant lot. It was a great place for hide-n-seek, especially behind all the old tires and junk stashed there. But Sally didn't want to play hide-n-seek now—and she couldn't see Homer or Zorch anywhere.

"Homer, Zorch, come!" Sally hoped the dogs would answer her call. Sure enough, a black lab head popped up from behind an old bedspring in the middle of the lot. Then Homer came bounding into sight. He ran to Sally and took her pant leg in his mouth.

"Homer, stop it," Sally said. "Hey, no nipping."

Homer kept at it, tugging Sally's pant leg and pulling her toward the bedsprings.

"Okay, okay, boy," Sally said. "Are you trying to show me something?"

Resolution

Sally followed Homer over to the far side of the bedsprings. There among the junk sat Zorch, feasting on Milky Bones—hundreds and hundreds of Milky Bones! But Zorch was not alone. With him was a scruffy dog with a filthy coat and no collar.

"Who are you, little fella?" Sally asked. "Whose doggy are you?"

The scruffy little dog sat back on his haunches and began to growl. But Zorch and Homer must have made some dog signal and their new friend backed off.

"Oh, I get it!" Sally exclaimed. "You're the Milky Bone thief and the Canine Crusaders have sniffed you out!"

"Don't worry, little guy. I'm not interested in your bones," Sally continued. "Now let's go home and tell the neighbors that the case of the missing Milky Bones is solved."

Sally, the crusaders, and Guy (as Sally came to name the scruffy little dog from the vacant lot) went home, steering clear of Mr. Grumpy's house, and frolicking all the way. Sally's dad went over to the lot after dinner with a wheelbarrow. He retrieved the stash of bones Guy had collected and redistributed them among the neighbors. Everyone laughed when they heard the story of the canine crusaders, and everyone came to love the new dogs in the neighborhood—just as much as, but not more than, Homer.

Creative Writing

Chapter 1 Writing Poetry

Forms of Poetry

Poems come in many forms. Some rhyme, some don't. Some are long, some short. Some are funny, some are sad. But all poetry has a special rhythm and form that sets it apart from prose or ordinary speech. Two of the most popular poem forms among students are ***haiku*** and ***limerick***.

HAIKU

A poem written in three lines. The first line is five syllables long, the second seven syllables long, and the last five syllables long. Most haiku is about nature.

The white herons flew
Over the vast blue ocean
They fly there no more

LIMERICK

A humorous poem written in five lines. The rhyme scheme is a a b b a. The first, second, and last lines each have three strong beats. The third and fourth lines each have two strong beats.

A pleasant young teacher from school, (a)
Not inclined to playing the fool, (a)
Tripped on an eraser, (b)
And fell without grace, "Er" (b)
She said, that young teacher from school. (a)

Poem Types and Terms

Ballad	A ***narrative poem*** that tells a story, often a sad one. Ballads, or ballades, have a tricky rhyme scheme. A literary ballad has three eight-line stanzas plus a quatrain at the end.
Blank verse	A poem in which the verses have a regular rhythm but do not rhyme.
Cinquain	A five-line stanza.
Couplet	A pair of lines that share something, usually rhythm and rhyme.
Elegy	A sad poem, most often written in honor of a dead person.
Epic	A long poem that tells a story, usually based on historic fact, about a hero and his actions. Homer's *Odyssey* is an example.
Lyric poem	A short, musical poem that expresses a feeling rather than tells a whole story.
Narrative poem	A poem that tells a story. It can be short or long.
Ode	A poem, often set to music, that has a theme of nobility or goodness.
Quatrain	A four-line stanza.
Sonnet	A love poem with a set rhyme scheme, written in 14 lines. Shakespeare wrote many sonnets.
Stanza	The paragraph of poetry. A stanza can be two lines long (as in a ***couplet***), three lines long (as in a ***haiku***), four lines long (as in a ***quatrain***), five lines long (as in a ***limerick***), or even 14 lines long (as in a ***sonnet***). The lines of a stanza share a set pattern, often a set meter, length, and rhyme scheme.

The First Poets

No one knows for sure who wrote the first poem. But we do know that ancient holy and wise people called ***shamans*** and ***druids*** created ***chants***. The chants were rhythmic strings of words used as prayers and spells. Today, chants still stir strong emotions.

Shamans and druids were very powerful people in their societies. They were treated almost as kings and queens. Druids in the Celtic culture were also the keepers of history. Young druids went to school for seven years, learning — by memory — the history of their people from older druids. The history was chanted in verse to help the storyteller remember the story and to keep listeners entertained. In later years, these druids became known as ***bards***. A bard is a singer or reciter of poetry.

Rhyme Schemes

Rhyme schemes are the patterns of rhyming words in poems. Rhyme schemes are written with small letters, beginning with ***a***.

Couplet

When at last the sun is set (a)
The fishers will haul in their net. (a)

ABAB

When at last the sun is set (a)
And the moon is risen **above** **(b)**
The fishers will haul in their net (a)
And peace will fly in with the **dove**. **(b)**

AABB

When at last the sun is set (a)
And the fishers have hauled in their net (a)
The moon will rise **above** **(b)**
And peace will fly in with the **dove**. **(b)**

Writing a Poem

1. Choose a topic for your poem.
2. Choose a form of poetry or create a rhyme scheme and the rhythm. Read over a few of your favorite poems to get started.
3. Form a picture in your mind to help you express your feelings colorfully and briefly. Write down a few similes or metaphors you may want to use in your poem.
4. Write a rough draft of your poem. Concentrate on expressing your ideas. You can fix the rhyme scheme and rhythm later.
5. Check the rhythm and, if necessary, the rhyme scheme. Then rewrite or revise, if necessary.

(See also Rough Draft to Final Copy, p. 76.)

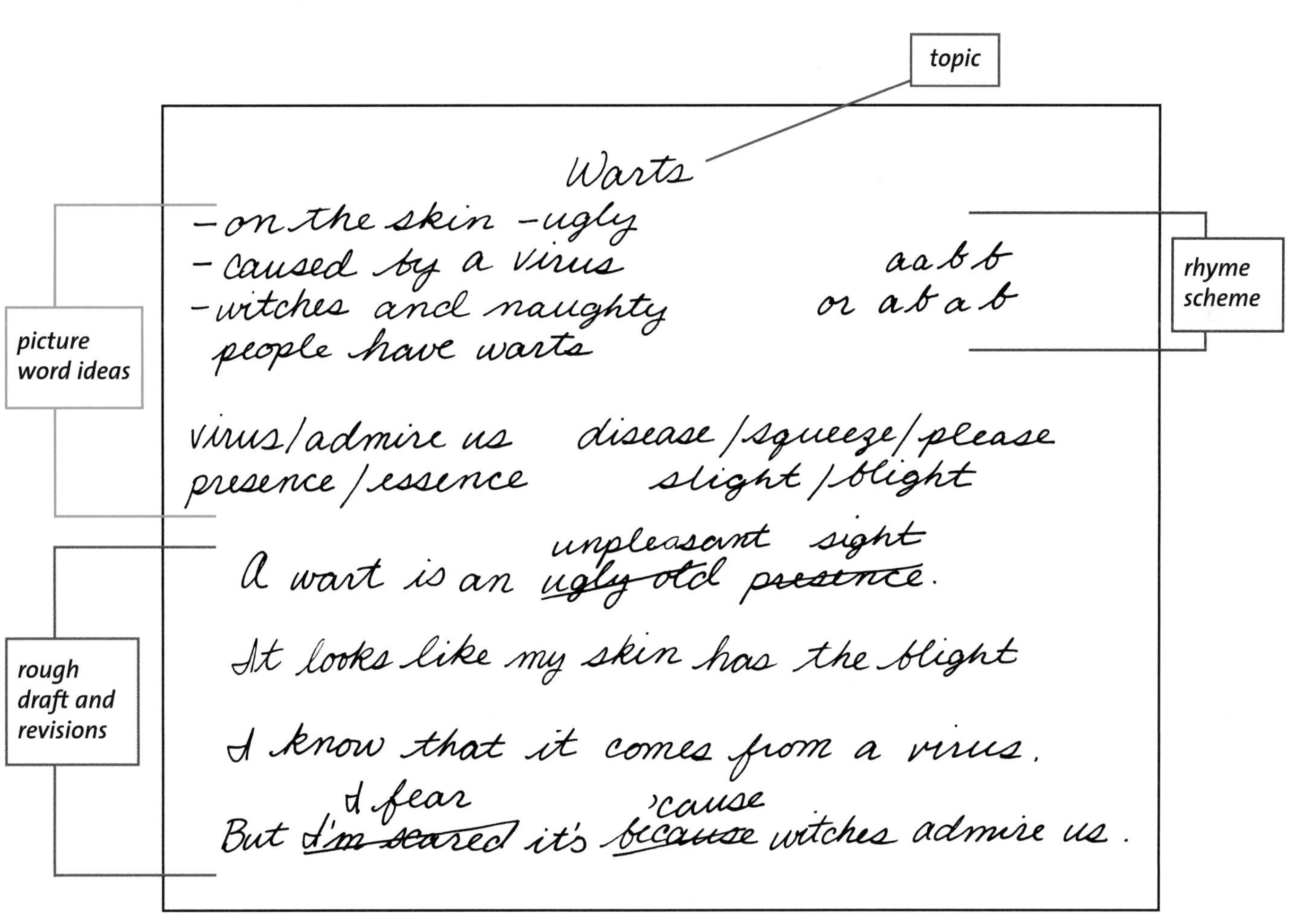

Chapter 2 Writing Prose Stories

Prose Story Forms

Prose stories come in two basic forms: novels and short stories. ***Novels*** are long stories, with distinct beginnings, middles, and ends. Novels are usually divided into several chapters, and they have characters, setting, and plot. Many novels use dialogue to allow characters to talk to each other. Prose stories are also called ***fiction***, something that is made up. Some writers create fiction entirely from their imaginations. Other writers create fiction based on real events or people.

Short stories also have beginnings, middles, and ends. They use characters, plot, and setting (see also Story Maps, p. 70).

Writing a Story

1. **Choose the kind of story you want to write: for example, a mystery, true adventure, romance, science fiction, or horror story. If you are writing a story with a historical setting or one that is based on a true story, be sure you have studied the facts. The more you know the history, the more real your story will seem.**
2. **Create a story map. List major characters, a setting, and a theme. Then outline the plot (the most important events) of the story.**
3. **Write a rough draft.**

Key Elements of Fiction

Good fiction is the result of the careful crafting of several elements. Among the most important of these elements are:

Characters **the people or main players in a story.**
Characters can be based on people you know or can be entirely made up. Characters must be believable or possess qualities that readers can understand or identify from their own experiences to make them seem real.

Plot **the story line, from beginning to end.**
The plot is the outline of the story's events. A plot can be simple or involve many twists and turns.

Setting **the location of the story.**
The setting is the place (or places) where the action of a story happens.

Dialogue **the words spoken by the character(s) in a story.**
Dialogue is used by many authors — especially by playwrights (see p. 95) — to develop characters, as well as to convey the events of the plot and details of setting.

Conflict **the source of dramatic tension in a story.**
Conflict is used to develop both plot and character(s). The conflict usually drives the plot in a story, and the resolution of the conflict is often the natural ending point of the story.

Theme **the main idea or message of a story.**
The theme of a story is usually described in the answers to one or more of the following questions:

- How did the main character change or what did he or she learn over the course of the story?
- What was the main feeling of the story?
- What idea(s) did the story impart? What was the story about?
- What did the author mean to say in telling the story?

Just What Kind of Prose Story Is It?
Glossary of Fiction Forms

Although some stories are difficult to describe, others fit neatly into standard categories:

Allegory A story in which the characters stand for ideas, such as Love, Pride, Greed, or Tolerance. The plot usually has a message or moral about real life.

Fable Like an allegory but short, with fewer characters and a simple moral. Aesop, a writer in ancient Greece, is probably the best-known ***fabulist***, or writer of fables.

Fairy Tale An adventure in which the heroes are often royalty or beloved by royalty and the villains are evil witches, sorcerers, or monsters.

Fantasy A tale set in an imaginary world with imaginary characters. For example, animals can talk and fairies roam the countryside in fantasies.

Historical Fiction Stories based on history, with fictional main characters. Historical fiction is sometimes set in real places and includes real people among its characters.

Horror Tales about scary things, from ghosts and goblins to monsters and murderers.

Informational Fiction A story or book that uses fictional characters or settings to tell about real things. For example, a story that explains science experiments might be told by a science teacher working in a fictional lab.

Legend An exaggerated story about a real person or event. For example, there is a story that George Washington, our first president, could never tell a lie.

Mystery Stories in which a problem is created by an unknown element. Mysteries are often crime stories. The main characters in mysteries are frequently detectives searching for a solution.

Myth A story made up to explain real events. Myths help us understand the beliefs and everyday life of the people described in them. Myths once were used to answer difficult questions, such as how the moon and stars came to be, why the seasons change, why the leopard has spots, etc. They also explained the relationships of human beings and gods. Almost every culture in the world has its own set of myths.

Realistic Fiction Stories with imaginary characters and events that are so believable that they could take place in the real world.

Romance Stories in which the main character or characters are looking for love and happiness. Some romances are historical and share many features of historical fiction.

Science Fiction Stories, often set in the future, that use elements of modern science. Some science fiction stories are set on other planets. Others tell of aliens landing on Earth or of computers that run the world.

Tall Tales Humorous stories that are full of exaggeration. Tall tales may or may not be about real people or events.

True Adventure Stories based on real people or real events, but the plot, setting, and characters are partly made up by the author.

Chapter 3 Writing Plays

Forms of Plays

A ***play*** is a story that is meant to be acted out. Like fiction, plays have characters, plots, and settings; beginnings, middles, and ends. The main difference is that, in a play, the story is told in dialogue and through the actions seen on a stage (which are written into the play as stage directions).

The author of a play is called a *playwright*. Some plays are short. Short plays are usually performed in one act and are called one-act plays. Longer plays consist of two or three acts.

Acts are like the chapters in a book. In performances, acts are usually separated by breaks called ***intermissions***. In plays of more than one act, the first act is called ***Act I***, the second act ***Act II***, etc. In most plays, acts are divided into ***scenes***. Scenes often require changes in time, setting, or characters on the stage. Scenes are numbered with small Roman numerals. The first scene in the second act of a play, for example, is written ***Act II*, *scene i***, or ***II*, *i***.

The Day the Ice Cream Truck Broke Down

Act I, scene i: Lights come up to show Jeff and Jamal sitting on a curb, their bikes resting beside them. They are dressed in summer clothes; a cap is backward on Jamal's head. Both boys look hot and tired.

Jeff: Some ride. I could really use a soda! Let's go to my house and get something to drink.

Jamal: I can't move—not even for soda. (Jamal takes off his cap, wipes sweat from his forehead with his other hand, replaces cap.) Gotta rest, Jeff, gotta rest.

DRAMA: A Brief History

Greek Drama

No one knows for certain when drama began. But we do know that more than 2,000 years ago, the Greeks presented powerful dramas that are still performed today.

In Greek theater, all the actors were men. Rather than use makeup, wigs, and costumes, the actors wore masks to fit their characters. Greek dramas also included a group of actors who stood on the side of the stage and chanted their reactions to the story. This group was called the ***chorus***.

Passion Plays

In the Middle Ages (800–1400), passion plays, dramas about the death of Jesus, were very popular in Europe. In addition to passion plays, other stories from the Bible were acted out, often in the town square on market days.

Shakespearean Theater

By the 1500s, the Bible was no longer the main source for play ideas. Historical plays and dramas about everyday life were also acted out.

Probably the most important playwright of this new era was William Shakespeare (1564–1616). In addition to writing 36 plays, he also built the Globe Theatre at Stratford-upon-Avon in England, the model for theaters ever since.

Chinese Theater

The theater in China took shape under the Yuan dynasty (1279–1368). The best-known form of drama today is the Beijing Opera, which became popular at the end of the 18th century. It combines dialogue and songs with dance, symbolic gestures, and acrobatics. The plays are based on Chinese history and folklore.

Japanese Theater

Not all dramas are acted out by using dialogue. Japanese Noh drama combines music and movement to tell a story. There is almost no scenery on the stage, and the actors wear masks and often elaborate costumes.

Other Forms of Drama

Mime is a dramatic form that uses movement and no dialogue to tell a story. ***Operas*** are dramas in which the characters sing the dialogue rather than speak it. ***Musical theater*** combines elements of plays with elements of opera so that characters speak and sing their roles. ***Puppet theater*** uses puppets instead of people to portray the characters in the play.

Writing a Play

1. Decide what you want your play to be about.
2. Create a story map. Choose characters, a setting, and a plot outline. Will your play have one, two, or three acts?
3. Write a rough draft of your play. Don't worry about the exact dialogue. Instead, write down the action and the main idea, what the characters are saying to each other, and the setting and mood of the story.
4. When you're pleased with the rough draft, write precise dialogue and stage directions.
5. Read your play out loud. How does the dialogue sound to you? To a listener?

(See also Rough Draft to Final Copy, p. 76.)

Scribing a Script:

Writing Down Dialogue and Stage Directions

Stage directions explain the setting and mood of a scene in a play. They also provide clues as to how the props, sets, and costumes should appear.

The Day the Ice Cream Truck Broke Down

Act I, scene i: Lights come up to show Jeff and Jamal sitting on a curb, their bikes resting beside them. They are dressed in summer clothes; a cap is backward on Jamal's head. Both boys look hot and tired.

Dialogue in a play is written by showing the name of the speaker first, followed by a colon:

Jeff: Some ride. I could really use a soda! Let's go to my house and get something to drink.

Jamal: I can't move—not even for soda. (Jamal takes off his cap, wipes sweat from his forehead with his other hand, replaces cap.) Gotta rest, Jeff, gotta rest.

Following the name of the speaker is the line or lines a character is to say.

Practical Writing

Journals

The word ***journal*** comes from the Latin word ***diurnalis***, which means day. A journal is another name for a ***daily diary***, a day-by-day account of events. Some people write in their journals every day, but you may decide to write less often, for example, once a week or whenever you feel you have something important to say.

Keeping a Journal

1. Decide if you want to keep a journal in which you write about your feelings and thoughts or one in which you record major events, or both.
2. Write the date at the top of the page.
3. Write down the most important things that happened on that day. You might want to explain why you think the events are important.
4. Every so often, review what you've written in your journal. You may want to continue or expand your thoughts on a particular day, or you may want to note how your thoughts and feelings may have changed.

May 31, 2005

Dear Diary,

Only two more weeks of school! I can hardly wait for summer vacation—no more pencils, no more books...

Mel and I got in an argument today. It was pretty stupid, but we patched it up. Mr. Hatcher gave us an assignment that included cutting pictures from magazines. I couldn't do it because Mel had my scissors. So I whispered to Mel to give them back. Mr. Hatcher told me to be quiet. Then I raised my hand, but Mr. Hatcher wouldn't call on me. Anyway, I told Mel off at recess and then he got mad. After a while I felt bad. He's more important than scissors!

Chapter 2

Letters

The ABCs of Letters

Letters come in two basic forms. ***Formal***, or ***business***, ***letters*** ask for and provide information. These letters are usually sent to strangers or acquaintances. ***Personal letters*** are sent between friends and relatives.

All Letters Have Five Basic Parts

1 Heading

A heading includes the date, your address, and, in a formal letter, the name and address of the person to whom you are writing.

2 Greeting

A greeting is a quick hello to the person receiving the letter. It usually begins with Dear. Be sure to capitalize the first letter in each word of the greeting. Put a comma at the end of the greeting in a personal letter, a colon in a business letter.

3 Body

The body is the main part of the letter. Many people indent the first line of the body. If you indent the first line, then indent the first line of every paragraph in the letter.

4 Closing

In a business letter, a closing can be Yours truly, Sincerely, or Regards. In a personal letter, you can write a familiar closing, for example, Your friend, Affectionately, or Love. Be sure to capitalize the first word of the closing and put a comma at the end of the closing.

5 Signature

Always sign your letter below the closing. In a formal letter, be sure to print or type your name beneath your signature.

Writing a Formal Letter

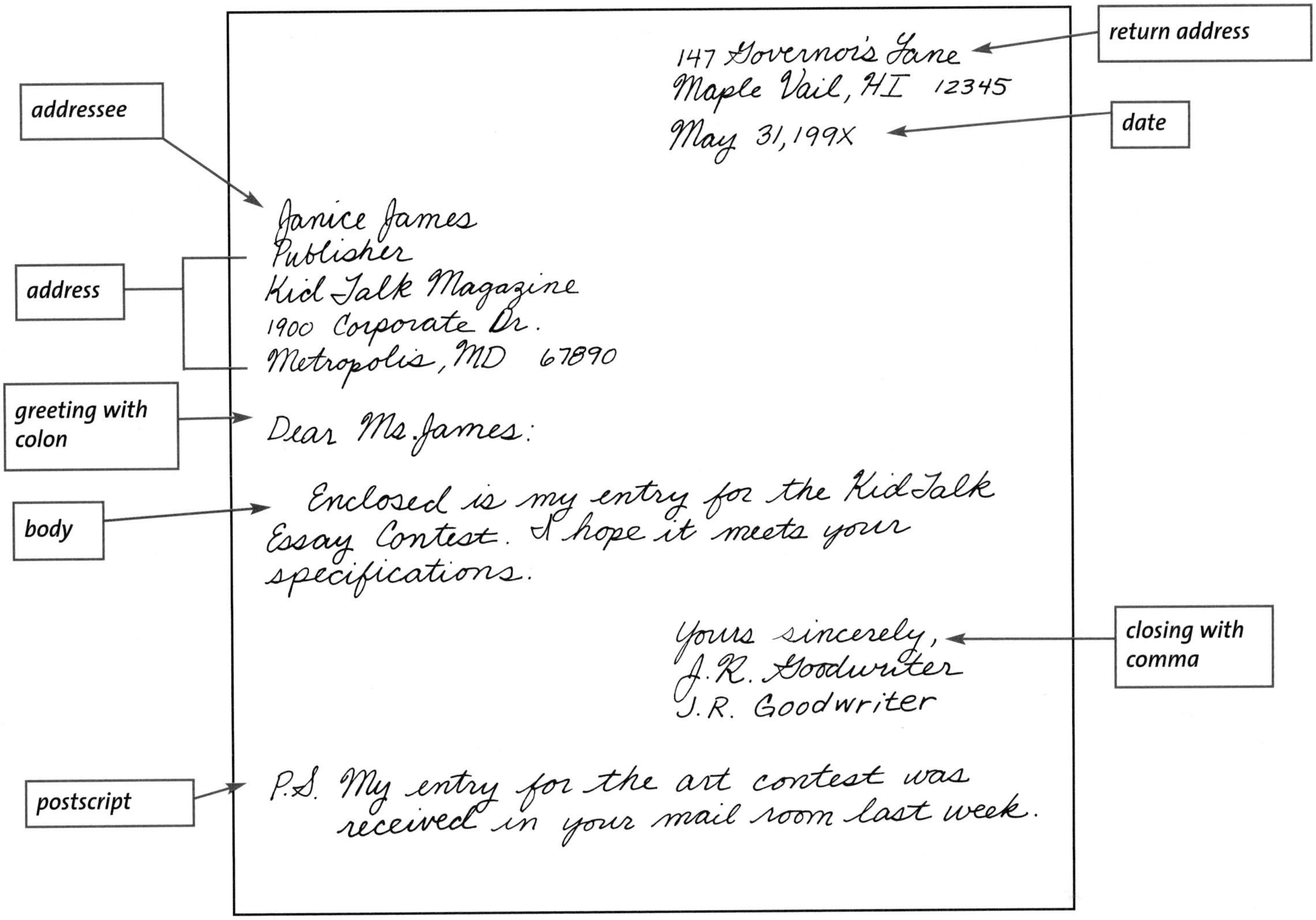

return address
147 Governor's Lane
Maple Vail, HI 12345
date
May 31, 199X
addressee
Janice James
address
Publisher
Kid Talk Magazine
1900 Corporate Dr.
Metropolis, MD 67890
greeting with colon
Dear Ms. James:
body
Enclosed is my entry for the Kid Talk Essay Contest. I hope it meets your specifications.
closing with comma
Yours sincerely,
J.R. Goodwriter
J.R. Goodwriter
postscript
P.S. My entry for the art contest was received in your mail room last week.

Addressing an Envelope

return address
My Name Here
111 Scholars Road
Thoughtful, KS 87965
place for stamp
address
U.R. Lettergetter
8910 Postal Ave.
Reading, FL 24153

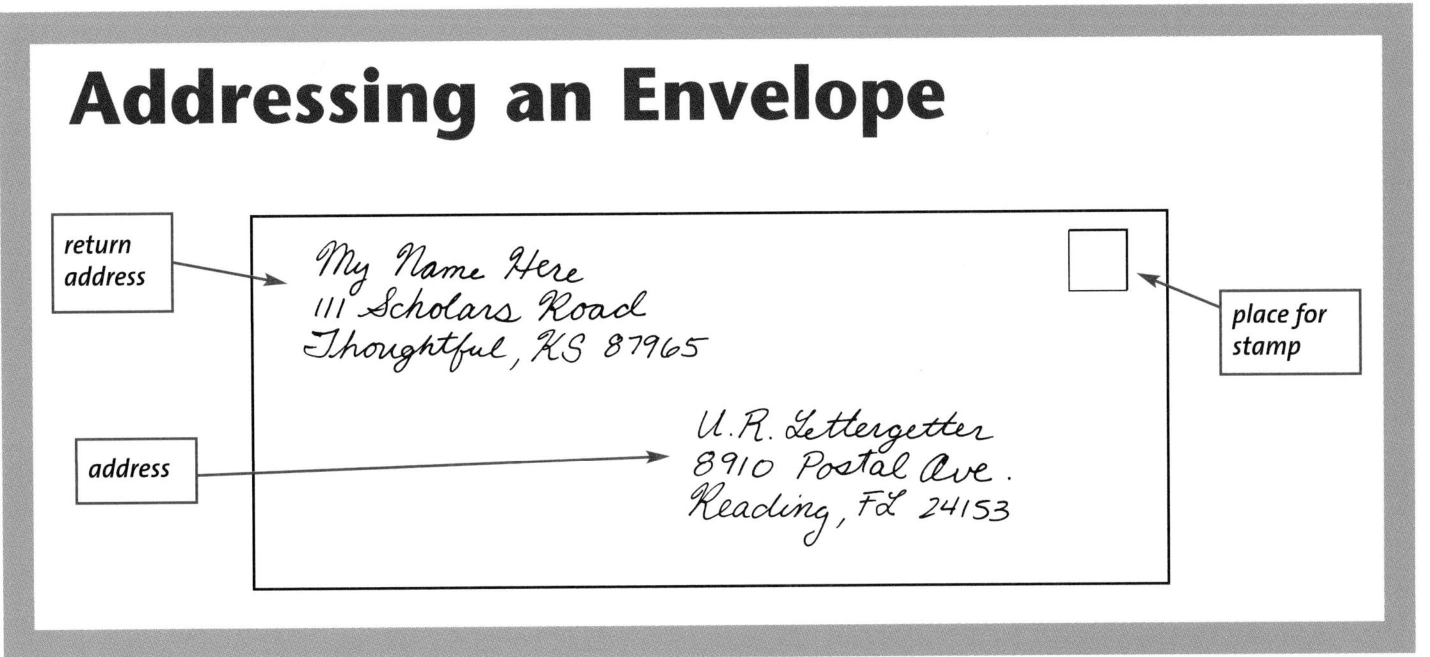

Writing a Personal Letter

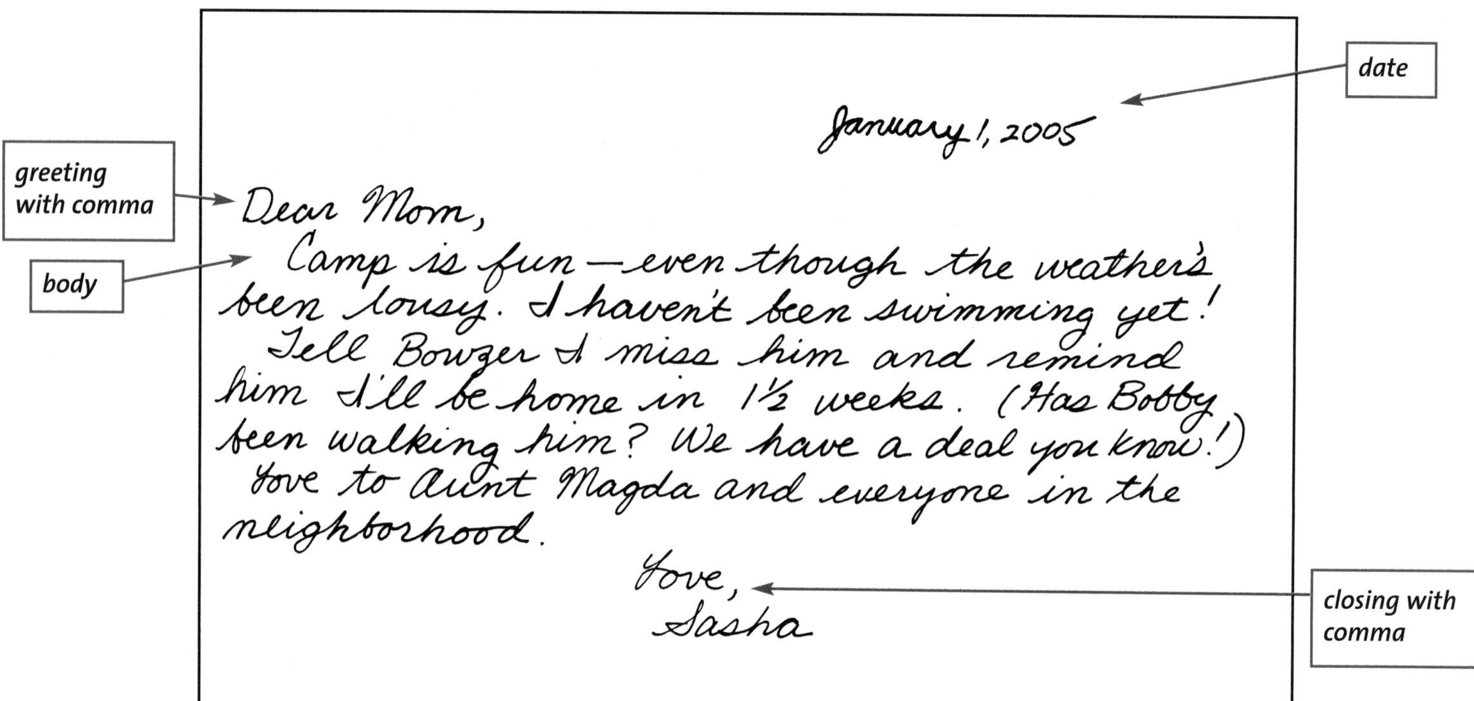
January 1, 2005

Dear Mom,

Camp is fun—even though the weather's been lousy. I haven't been swimming yet!

Tell Bowzer I miss him and remind him I'll be home in 1½ weeks. (Has Bobby been walking him? We have a deal you know!)

Love to Aunt Magda and everyone in the neighborhood.

Love,

Sasha

A Party? Writing Invitations

Invitations can be written on sheets of folded paper or on little squares of card stock. They can be formal or casual, colorful or plain. Invitations should always include four pieces of information:

1. **Type of event (birthday party, surprise party, holiday theme party, costume party, club meeting, and so on)**
2. **Time**
3. **Date**
4. **Place**

If you're serving food, you might want to add RSVP to the invitations. RSVP stands for *répondez s'il vous plaît*, and means "please respond." If you add RSVP be sure to supply a phone number or address so invitees will know how to respond.

Type of Event: Birthday

Time: 6:00 PM

Date: Saturday, June 10th

Place: Susan's house
123 Deer Run

RSVP: 555-1234

Chapter 3 Essays

Essays express personal opinions. You can write an essay about any topic or theme that you feel strongly about. Your essay may describe your feelings about the quality of food in the school cafeteria or why you love summer camp. Anything that stirs your emotions is probably a good essay topic.

To write an effective essay, you have to describe your opinions and ideas so that your readers can understand them. It's not enough to say that the food is awful or that camp is terrific. You need to back up your opinion with details so your readers will understand your point of view. You can use argument, humor, or exaggeration to make your points.

Essays are made up of four parts:
1. Title
2. Introduction
3. Body
4. Conclusion

Writing an Essay

1. Choose a topic.
2. Outline the major points of your opinion (see Outlines, pp. 68–69).
3. Write a rough draft of your essay. The introduction should state the topic of your essay and your opinion on the topic. The body should list the reasons you feel as you do about your topic and offer any additional information or experiences to support your opinion. The conclusion should summarize the reasons you listed in the body of your essay and persuade your readers to share your opinion.

Be sure to choose an essay topic that's manageable. For example, rather than write about "Sports and Kids," consider writing about "The Pressure on Kids to Win at Sports."

What's the Point? Different Types of Essays

Essays can be short or long, serious or witty, based purely in fact or in personal opinion. However, most essays fall into three distinct categories: ***expository***, ***persuasive***, and ***humorous***.

Expository essays explain or describe, and are also called ***explanatory*** essays and ***descriptive*** essays.

Persuasive essays are written to convince or persuade readers to adopt the writer's point of view.

Humorous essays can be either expository or persuasive, but use humor to bring home the message.

Chapter 4 Reports

Reports are factual compositions. They describe the facts about anything—events, places, people, animals, plants, planets, stars, products, and more.

Writing a Report

1 Choose a topic.

2 Gather a variety of resource and reference materials. Be sure you can find enough information to use in your report. If you find too much information, narrow down the subject of your report.

3 Take notes. As you read through the reference and resource materials, write down the most important information and interesting facts. Be sure to keep track of the information and its sources. You'll need this for the bibliography (see p. 111).

4 Write an outline (see Outlines, pp. 68–69). Put all the information and interesting facts from your notes into an organized framework.

5 Write a rough draft. Incorporate as much information as you can from your outline and notes. The introduction should tell the topic of your report. The body should include important information and interesting facts. The conclusion should summarize the main points from the body.

6 Revise your report. Be sure the information in each of the paragraphs belongs together. Check to see that one paragraph flows smoothly into the next.

(See Rough Draft to Final Copy, p. 76.)

Research on the Internet

The Internet provides a link to valuable research resources. In order to use the Internet, work through a search engine or portal that allows you to access the World Wide Web.

Most search engines have a "search" command on their home pages (the main screens that appear when you log on to the search engines). Type in a key word or words and click on "search." Once the search is completed, a listing of sources will be provided on the screen.

If too many responses result from your initial search, define your search more narrowly. For example, if you were writing a report on breeds of Siamese cats in your state, you may have to type in "Siamese cats" as your search term. The chances are good that several hundred or more responses would result from your search. Next, try adding a keyword to the search, perhaps, "Siamese cats, Tennessee," and see if you get a more manageable number of resources in response.

If your search produces few or no responses, try to broaden it. For example, if your initial search was defined as "Siamese cats, Palmerston," you might broaden your search by trying "Siamese cats, Tennessee."

Note that good research practice means citing Internet sources just as you would book, magazine, newspaper, or interview sources. Be sure to credit Internet sources by listing Web sites and Internet authors as part of your bibliographies and reference lists (see p. 111).

Using the Library to Research Your Report

You might have an encyclopedia at home or some books you can use to gather information for a report. But chances are you need to find additional material—so you go to the library. But how do you find the information you need in all those shelves of books? By using the card catalog or computer indexing system. The card catalog or computer index in most libraries is sorted into three categories:

1. **Subject**
2. **Author**
3. **Title**

Within each category, resources are sorted alphabetically. If you know the author of a book or periodical you need for research, use the author index. If you know the title, try the title index. If you don't know the author or the title, you can find information by looking up the subject you're interested in. Just go to the subject index and take a look around.

Some computer indexes allow you to search by keywords that can be typed into a search screen. Use as many keywords as you can to narrow your search for the best sources for your research.

REVIEWS:
Cross Between Essay and Report

Reviews combine ingredients of both essays and reports to give the facts—and then express an opinion.

Book reports are one kind of review. When you write a book report, you summarize the main events of the story and describe the characters, setting, and plot. You can describe the things you like or dislike about the book, as long as you make it clear that you're stating your opinion.

Reviews are written every day about everything from cars to toys, movies to music. Look in your local newspaper. You'll probably find a review or two.

NONFICTION: Getting Real

Nonfiction takes on different forms and different topics, depending on the writer and the reasons for writing. Some reports fill entire books or fulfill a particular purpose. These special reports have special names.

Autobiography A story of the author's life.

Biography A story of a person's life written by another person.

Essay A nonfiction story that discusses one topic or theme from a personal point of view (see p. 103).

History An account of a past event or era.

Journal A diary or record of day-to-day events (see p. 98).

News Stories Reports written in a special format, usually used in newspapers and magazines (see p. 109).

Reference A collection of useful facts and information organized for quick study rather than for leisurely reading.

Travelogue Nonfiction writing, often in the style of a journal or a news story, that tells about a journey or trip to a particular place.

Better Book Reports: A Seven-Step Plan

GETTING STARTED

1 **Select a book that interests you. Look at the cover.**
Then read the title and the description on the book cover. If the book still seems interesting, open it. Are there pictures? Read a paragraph or two. Are you still interested? If not, try another book.

2 **Read the book—all of it.**

GETTING DOWN TO BUSINESS

3 **Take notes for the first draft of your book report.**
Write down the title, author, and genre (novel, history, biography, and so on) of the book. Then note the names of the major characters and the setting. Next, take notes on the main events, the problem (or conflict) in the book, and its solution. Last, describe one or two favorite episodes from the book.

4 **Organize your notes and start your first draft.**
Write down the title and author of the story. Then, write a one- to three-paragraph summary of the book. Don't retell every little detail or episode. Instead, limit your summary to the most important events in the story. Next, describe the problem or conflict in the story and how that problem is solved. This is especially important in writing a book report on a novel or piece of fiction. Last, give your opinion of the story and why you feel the way you do.

5 **Read over your draft.**
Try reading it aloud, and ask a friend or family member to read it, too. Note the parts that you want to revise.

FINISHING UP

6 **Edit your book report.**
Reread your edited draft. Are you happy with it? Should you revise it even more, or are you satisfied with your work?

7 **When you're finished with your draft, write a neat, final copy of your book report.**

FANCY THOUGHTS

You may want to draw a picture of a scene from the book to include with the report. You might create an illustrated cover or choose to display your book report on a poster with several drawings. Perhaps you'd like to create a filmstrip about the book, one that includes your report and a series of illustrations for each part. Be creative!

Chapter 5 News Stories

News stories are factual stories that usually have a special structure called a ***pyramid***. The structure is called a pyramid because the first part of the story tells just the main facts. Then, as the story continues, the facts are described in greater detail to "widen" the story gradually to its "base," or conclusion. A good news story answers the questions ***who***, ***what***, ***when***, ***where***, ***how***, and sometimes ***why***.

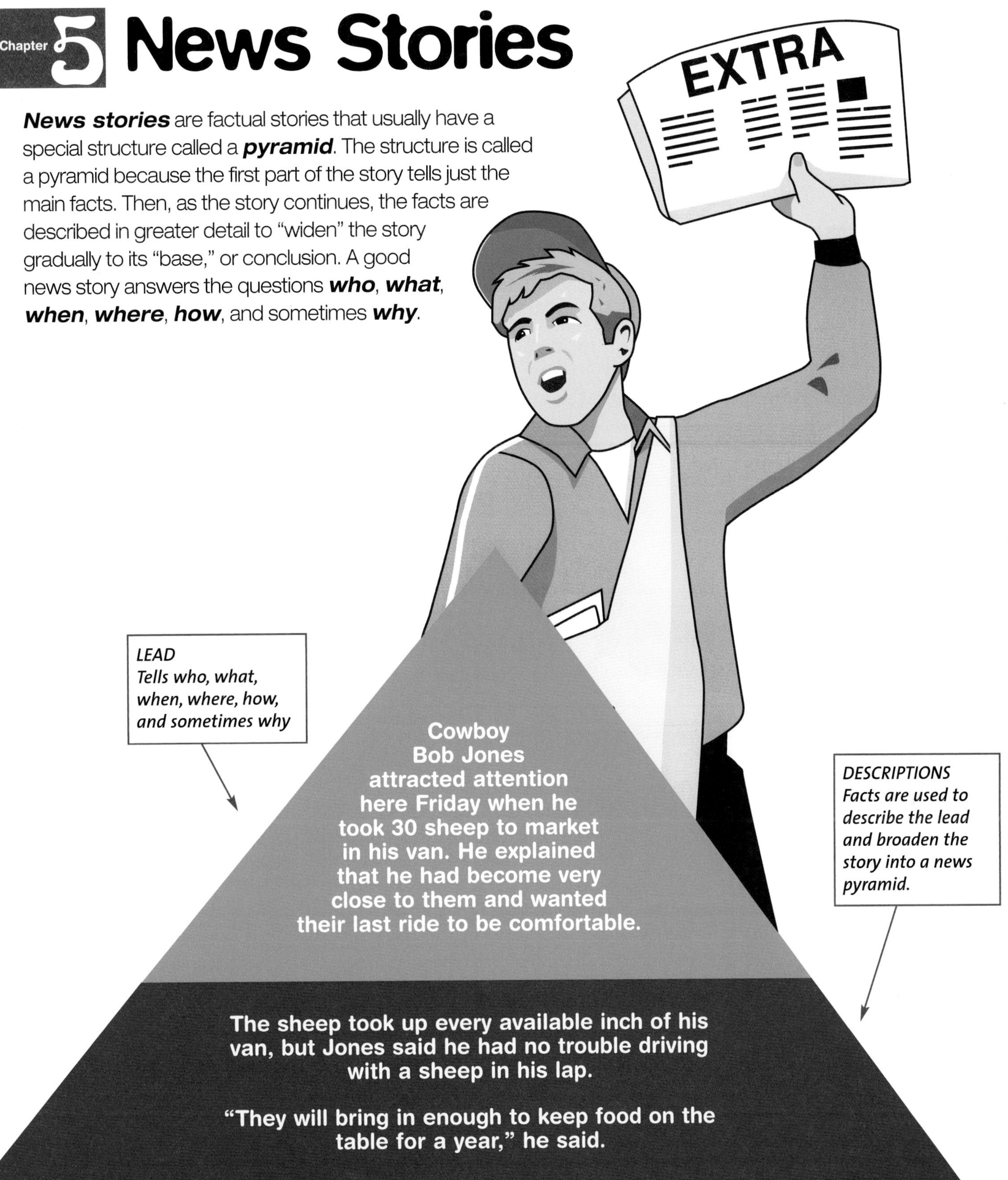

PRACTICAL WRITING

EXTRA! EXTRA!
READ ALL ABOUT IT!

Dateline

Headline

Masthead

Photo illustration

Caption

Headline

Cutline

Index

STUDENT NEWS

Volume 1, No. 1

Mid-November Edition

Unwelcome boosters spotted at pep rally

Presley President

J. R. Presley clobbered the competition in the student council presidential election held last Tuesday, Election Day. Presley won 73 percent of the votes cast by Palmerston Elementary students.

Longer Lunch

Presley attributes her landslide victory to her "longer lunch" platform.

"Our lunch period was cut this year from 20 minutes to 15. It's tough to get your lunch from the cafeteria line, take your seat, eat, and bus your tray in that time," Presley said.

In her campaign speech, Presley promised to negotiate with Principal McSwiney to restore the lost five minutes to the lunch schedule for all grades.

Bats Cause Queasy Feelings at Palmerston Pep Rally

Oct. 31.—Bats are living in the Palmerston Elementary gym, according to maintenance engineer I. M. Scarett, who discovered the bats this morning. "There must be 50 or so hanging right behind the stage curtain on the north side of the gym," he reported. Scarett's discovery explains the moving shadows and odd whooshing noises reported in the gym at the evening pep rally on October 28.

Following the rally, student and teacher pep club members asked Palmerston maintenance to investigate the peculiar atmosphere in the gym.

"I sensed an odd presence," 5th grader Sarah Chandler remarked, "and heard kind of a low, beating sound, kind of a 'whoosh, whoosh' sound."

Amar Turk, a 4th grader, added, "The lights were weird. Shadows kept crossing the gym floor. But when I looked up, I didn't see anything. Just more shadows!"

Maintenance director Euby Comfort at first suspected the eerie effects were caused by a problem in the air circulation system. But Scarett, while investigating the air ducts on the gym stage, discovered a more likely culprit.

"Those bats were probably flying around behind the sheer stage curtain the night of the rally," Comfort concluded. Scarett added, "That sure would make one scary shadow play!"

Writing a News Story

1 Gather facts.

Be sure you can answer the questions ***who***, ***what***, ***when***, ***where***, and ***how***. Take notes. If possible, interview people who are involved in the story or who are experts on your subject. Be sure you write down the exact words of the people you plan to quote.

2 Write a lead.

A lead is the first sentence or paragraph in a news story. Think of it as the tip of the pyramid. It tells the basic ideas of the story and gets the reader interested.

3 Write the body of the story.

The body fills in details about the lead.

4 Write a headline for your story.

Try to make the headline a catchy title, one that hints at the action in the news story.

Credit Where Credit Is Due:
Writing References and Bibliographies

A ***bibliography*** shows where you got the information for a report. It is a list of articles, books, or other sources.

Bibliographies are organized alphabetically by the author's last name or, when there is no author named, by the name of the publication. Then the title is listed, followed by the name of the publisher. The place and date of publication are listed at the end.

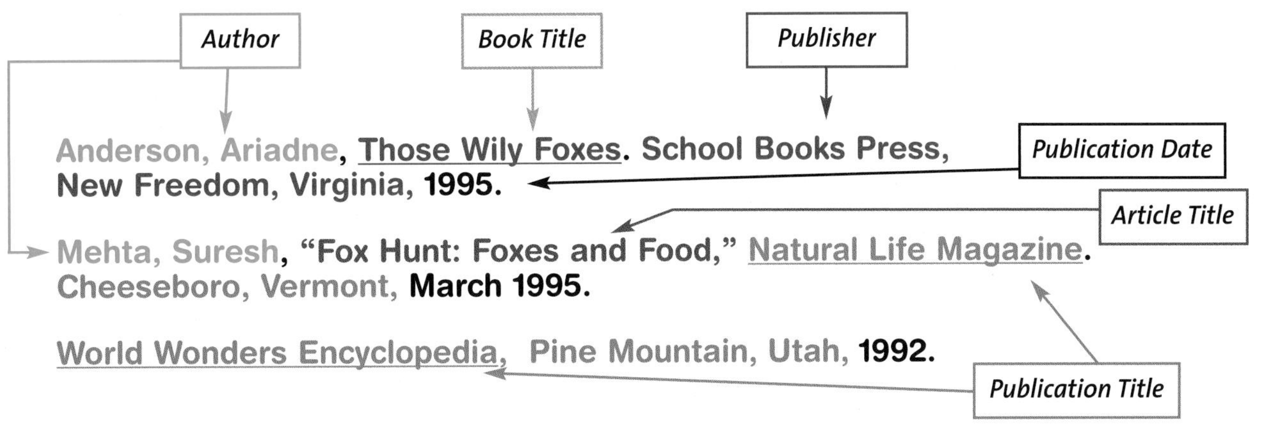

Chapter 1 Reading Comprehension

Reading comprehension, or how well you understand what you read, is a very important skill for all your school classes, not just English class. So how can you get the most out of your reading and improve your reading comprehension?

Many educators and authors have devised plans to help students improve their reading skills. An approach called ***SQR3*** is especially popular. SQR3 means

Survey
Question
Read
Recite
Review

SURVEY

To survey means to skim through or scan what you are about to read to get a general idea about the material.

QUESTION

To question means to reason what the author is trying to say in the material. Is the meaning literal? That is, is the author's message conveyed directly in the words he or she uses? Or is the meaning inferential? Does the author say one thing as a symbol for something else?

The family was in the middle of a raging storm.

READ

Once you've surveyed the material and questioned the purpose of the writing, you're ready to read the material word for word. This will reinforce or clarify the impressions gained from your survey and questioning, and will reinforce the details of the story and the author's intention in writing it.

RECITE

After reading the material, recite in your own words what the author has said in the passage.

REVIEW

If you have difficulty, reread the material to pick up on the details or ideas that you missed in the first reading.

Chapter 2 Expressions

Expressions are words or phrases that are used to convey ideas or feelings beyond their dictionary definitions. Expressions color our thoughts and ideas and provide writers with a shortcut to explaining a complex concept or feeling. Some expressions relate ideas to historical events or people, others to myths, legends, or the Bible.

Many authors use expressions in their books and articles. That means you need to understand the expressions in order to understand their writing.

Adages, Proverbs, and Maxims

Adages, ***proverbs***, and ***maxims*** are sayings that have been used for many years that tell truths about life or human nature. For example:

A stitch in time saves nine.

If you sew up a tear when it requires only one stitch to fix, the tear won't get bigger and require a greater effort — nine stitches — to fix later. This expression means that if you pay attention to problems and solve them early, they won't become bigger problems later on.

Clichés

Clichés are sayings that have been used too much to make a strong impression. Clichés should be avoided in writing and speaking. For example:

That person is as odd as a three-dollar bill.

Because there is no such thing as a three-dollar bill, the person is odd or silly.

Expressions from History, Literature, and the Bible

Achilles' heel A weak spot. In Greek mythology, Achilles was a hero whose only weak spot was on his heel. He was unbeatable in battle until an arrow finally struck him in the heel.

In school, math was his Achilles' heel.

Add insult to injury Make a bad situation worse. In a fable by Aesop (see p. 94), a man swats at a fly that has bitten him on his head. Instead of hitting the fly, he hits himself on his sore head. The fly muses that the man has "added insult to injury" by making more pain for himself unnecessarily.

By insisting he was not stealing when he was caught with the merchandise, John simply added insult to injury.

Baker's dozen Thirteen, or a little extra. This expression dates back to 1266 in England. Laws were passed by Parliament to protect people from bakers who offered small loaves of bread. To ensure that they met the government standards for weight, the bread bakers threw in an extra loaf per dozen (or 12) sold.

He gave me a baker's dozen of cupcakes.

Cry wolf Call for help when there's no danger. About 2,500 years ago, Aesop wrote a story about a shepherd boy who was protecting a flock of sheep from a wolf. The boy was bored and decided to call out as if the wolf were threatening the sheep to see if someone would come. So he cried, "Wolf!" Sure enough, the village people came running to help the boy protect the sheep. When they discovered the wolf was not around, they were annoyed and returned home. But as the days went by, the boy grew more bored and again cried, "Wolf!" The villagers came again and were even more annoyed when they found the boy was bluffing. They went home. Then one day a wolf really did come. The boy called out, "Wolf! Wolf!" But no one came. The villagers thought he was bluffing. The moral: If you keep telling lies, no one will believe you, even when you tell the truth!

He's always crying wolf, so I can't believe he really has a headache.

Drop in the bucket An amount that doesn't matter. In the Bible, the prophet Isaiah explains that God has created a vast universe. He continues to say that the nations of the world are but drops in the bucket by comparison — unimportant.

This worksheet is a drop in the bucket compared with the three tests coming up next week!

Eat humble pie Apologize for making an error. The original expression was to eat ***umble*** pie. Umble — the heart, liver, and intestines of deer — used to be cooked up in pies for poor people while the wealthy enjoyed the loins and ribs of the animal.

When she proved I was wrong, I ate humble pie.

Go whole hog Stop at nothing. Eating pork was against the religious laws of Judaism and Islam, although religious scholars often puzzled over whether it was only certain parts of the hog that could not be eaten. To go whole hog was to forget about the laws and splurge.

I sure went whole hog when I spent all my allowance on that video game!

Idioms

Idioms are sayings whose meanings can't be understood from the individual words in them. For example:

Apple of one's eye The "apple of one's eye" is not an apple in a person's eye. It is a favorite person. The idiom comes from the idea that an apple is a beautiful thing to see and promises to hold good things inside. A favorite person is always pleasant to see and well-loved—that is, good inside.

Herbert's daughter, Wendy, is the apple of his eye.

Greek to me Too difficult to understand. In the Shakespeare play *Julius Caesar*, the Romans speak Greek when they want to keep their messages secret. One of the Romans, a fellow named Casca, is asked if he'd heard some important news. He says, ". . . for mine part, it was Greek to me." Casca had no idea what was said.

My sister studies algebra, but it's Greek to me.

In the doghouse In trouble and being punished. In *Peter Pan*, Mr. Darling treats Nana harshly. His children are angry with him, so he sits in Nana's doghouse until they'll speak to him again.

Dom has been in the doghouse with Mom ever since he left his new bike in the rain.

John Hancock Your signature. John Hancock was an American patriot and the first signer of the Declaration of Independence. He wrote his name especially large at the bottom of the Declaration to make sure it could be seen.

They put their John Hancocks on the petition to save the whales.

Mad as a hatter Crazy. Hatters, or milliners, used mercury to treat the felt fabric used for hats. The mercury gave many of the hatters a severe twitch, which made it impossible for them to work, much less act normally. The Mad Hatter is a well-known character in *Alice's Adventures in Wonderland.*

Stay away from that guy. He's mad as a hatter.

(Open) Pandora's box Ask for trouble. In Greek mythology, Pandora was given a box by Zeus, who told her she must never open it because it contained everything bad in the world—illness, sadness, gloom, and misery. But curiosity got the best of Pandora. She opened the box and released all the ills on the world.

When the principal asked for criticisms, she really opened Pandora's box.

Read between the lines Guess at the real meaning of things, or the truth behind what is written. Before paper was common, books and official documents were written on parchment made from animal skins. Parchment was very valuable. Rather than throw it away if the messages on it were old, it was reused. The old ink was covered over to make a clear page for another document. On some old parchment, you can actually "read between the lines" because the writing underneath shows through.

She said the rock star was out of the country, but, if you read between the lines, she probably was just saying that so he wouldn't have to talk to reporters.

Slow and steady wins the race Aesop's fable "The Tortoise and the Hare" tells about a race between a tortoise and a hare (rabbit). The hare teases the tortoise, but the tortoise keeps going. The hare is so confident that he will win the race that he stops for a nap. As he sleeps, the tortoise, slowly but surely, crosses the finish line first.

Chonra studied a little every night last week for her social studies test. Kendra crammed the night before. Kendra wrote ten wrong answers, and Chonra wrote only one. Slow and steady wins the race.

Sour grapes Fools dislike what they cannot have. In Aesop's fable "The Fox and the Grapes," a fox passes a vineyard and spies some tasty-looking grapes. He jumps the fence and tries to grasp the grapes in his jaw, but they are out of reach. The fox tries again and again, but still cannot claim the prized grapes. At last the fox stomps off toward home, saying, "Who needs those grapes? They're probably sour anyway."

After Ferdie's team lost the soccer match, he said the other team cheated, but I think it was just sour grapes.

Wolf in sheep's clothing Someone or something that isn't what it appears to be. In one of Aesop's fables, a wolf puts on a sheepskin in order to blend in with a flock of sheep—the easier to kill the sheep for his supper. But the shepherd has the last laugh. He thinks the wolf is a sheep and kills him for his own supper.

K.C. said she was joining our team because she liked us better, but I'm afraid she may be a wolf in sheep's clothing.

Appendix: Some Good Books to Read

FICTION

ADVENTURE

Black Duck
by Janet Taylor Lisle
Ruben finds rumrunners, crime bosses, gangs, and a disappearing dead man in this Prohibition tale of suspense and intrigue. Philomel

Harry Potter series
by J. K. Rowling
Using spells, strategy, and inner strength, boy wizard Harry Potter battles Lord Voldemort in his quest to avenge the deaths of his parents and secure peace for all. Scholastic

Holes
by Louis Sachar
In this Newbery-winning novel, Stanley Yelnats is sent to a boys' juvenile detention center in the Texas desert. As punishment, every day the boys must dig holes, five feet deep and five feet across. Random House

The Mysterious Benedict Society
by Trenton Lee Stewart
Highly gifted children are selected to infiltrate the Learning Institute for the Very Enlightened, an organization attempting to brainwash the public and take over the world. Little, Brown

Peak
by Roland Smith
After fourteen-year-old Peak Marcello is arrested for scaling a Manhattan skyscraper, a judge orders him to leave the city with his mountaineer father, who pushes him to become the youngest person to climb Mount Everest. Harcourt

Secret Letters From 0 to 10
by Susie Morgenstern
Ernest's life is very dull until he meets Victoria. Puffin

Slake's Limbo
by Felice Holman
This is the story of a thirteen-year-old boy and how he survives living under New York City's Grand Central Station. Simon & Schuster

Spirit Quest
by Susan Sharpe
Aaron and his new friend Robert find adventure on a Spirit Quest, a Native American wilderness experience. Sagebrush Education

Take Me to the River
by Will Hobbs
In this river adventure, two determined boys make their way down the Rio Grande by canoe and raft, but severe weather and border troubles may force them to change course. HarperCollins

The Tale of Despereaux: Being the Story of a Mouse, a Princess, Some Soup, and a Spool of Thread
by Kate DiCamillo
This Newbery-winning novel tells the intertwined stories of Despereaux Tilling, a mouse who falls deeply in love with Princess Pea; Chiaroscuro the Rat; and the girl Miggery Sow. Candlewick Press

Tunnels
by Brian Williams and Roderick Gordon
When Will searches for answers about the disappearance of his archaeologist father, he discovers an underground world . . . and more danger than he ever imagined. Scholastic

Woods Runner
by Gary Paulsen
British soldiers burn Samuel's house to the ground. He embarks on a dangerous mission to find his parents, who have been taken captive as prisoners of war. Wendy Lamb Books

FANTASY AND SCIENCE FICTION

Dark Life
by Kat Falls
Ty has spent his entire life living in a colony under the sea. When outlaws attack his home, he and a topsider named Gemma band together to uncover secrets and defeat the enemy. Scholastic

The Giver
by Lois Lowry
Given his lifetime assignment in the Ceremony of Twelve, Jonas becomes the receiver of memories shared by only one other in his community and learns the terrible truth about the society in which he lives. (Newbery Medal) Houghton

Help! I'm Trapped in Obedience School
by Todd Strasser
Jack accidentally turns his best friend into a dog. Scholastic

The Hunger Games
by Suzanne Collins
As a contestant in an annual televised fight to the death, Katniss is determined to outwit the other players . . . and the creators of the game. Scholastic

It's All Greek to Me
by Jon Scieszka
As they are about to go onstage, Joe, Fred, and Sam are transported back to the time of Zeus and the other gods in Greek mythology, who, strangely enough, behave much as the characters in the trio's class play. Puffin

King of Shadows
by Susan Cooper
While working in a replica of the famous Globe Theatre in London, Nat finds himself transported back to 1599 and performing in the original theater under the guidance of Shakespeare himself. Simon & Schuster

The Lost Flower Children
by Janet Taylor Lisle
Olivia and Nellie find wonder and hope in their great-aunt's garden, which is filled with fabulous characters and deep emotions. Putnam

Monster of the Month Club
by Dian Curtis Regan
Rilla thinks her stuffed monsters are cute—until they start to wake up! Scholastic

Mrs. Frisby and the Rats of NIMH
by Robert C. O'Brien
An intriguing story about a race of superrats created by the scientists at NIMH. Aladdin

Nosepickers from Outer Space
by Gordon Korman
Fourth-grader Devin's disappointment in the nerdy live-in exchange student changes to amazement when he realizes that the "nerd" is an alien who communicates home through his nose! Disney Press

Percy Jackson series
by Rick Riordan
Percy Jackson, who discovers that he's the son of Poseidon, suddenly finds himself embroiled in a war among the Greek gods. Hyperion

The Phantom Tollbooth
by Norton Juster
Milo embarks on an exciting adventure in a strange country of edible words and mysterious creatures, fabulous wit and wordplay. Random House

Shadow Children series
by Margaret Peterson Haddix
In this future society, shadow children—any children over the legal family limit of two—are often killed or imprisoned. But the shadow children band together to save themselves and overthrow the government that seeks to destroy them. Simon & Schuster

Skellig
by David Almond
Unhappy about his baby sister's illness and his move into a dilapidated old house, Michael retreats to the backyard shed, where he discovers a strange, owl-like man. Random House

The Trolls
by Polly Horvath
Aunt Sally tells stories about strange relatives and trolls. Farrar, Straus & Giroux

The World's Worst Fairy Godmother
by Bruce Coville
Why is Maybelle considered the world's worst fairy godmother? Maybe it's her secret enemy.... Simon & Schuster

HISTORICAL FICTION

Al Capone Does My Shirts
by Gennifer Choldenko
Because his father works at the prison, twelve-year-old Moose lives on Alcatraz, where gangster Al Capone is held. Between caring for his autistic sister and being friends with the prison warden's daughter, Moose has his hands full. Could Capone help? (Newbery Honor) Putnam

Catherine, Called Birdy
by Karen Cushman
The thirteen-year-old daughter of an English country knight records her struggle to escape the usual role of women in her time and place. HarperCollins

Chasing Lincoln's Killer
by James L. Swanson
This historical thriller describes the suspenseful twelve-day manhunt for John Wilkes Booth, Abraham Lincoln's assassin. Scholastic

Crispin: The Cross of Lead
by Avi
This Newbery-winning novel transports readers back to fourteenth-century England, where a young serf on the run from his miserable past comes to discover not only his true identity but also a sense of self-worth. Hyperion

Esperanza Rising
by Pam Muñoz Ryan
After a family tragedy forces her to flee from Mexico to the United States with her mother, Esperanza, who's always been treated like a princess, has to become a farm worker. Scholastic

The Evolution of Calpurnia Tate
by Jacqueline Kelly
Calpurnia Tate, age eleven, would rather explore the woods and collect scientific data than cook and do needlework, but a girl growing up at the turn of the twentieth century might not have a choice. (Newbery Honor) Square Fish

The Keeping Room
by Anna Myers
Left in charge of his family during the Revolutionary War, thirteen-year-old Joey's view of what is right and wrong changes. Will his father feel betrayed? Puffin

A Long Way from Chicago
by Richard Peck
A boy recounts his annual summer trips to rural Illinois with his sister during the Great Depression. The kids visit their larger-than-life grandmother. Puffin

Love from Your Friend, Hannah
by Mindy Warshaw Skolsky
It is 1937. Hannah's best friend has moved away and she is looking for a pen pal. HarperCollins

Miss Spitfire
by Sarah Miller
Annie Sullivan accepts a seemingly impossible task—she agrees to teach a blind and deaf young woman named Helen Keller. Atheneum

Number the Stars
by Lois Lowry
In 1943, during the German occupation of Denmark, ten-year-old Annemarie learns how to be brave when she helps shelter her Jewish friends from the Nazis. (Newbery Medal) Bantam

Out of the Dust
by Karen Hesse
In a series of poems, fifteen-year-old Billie Jo relates the hardships of living on her family's wheat farm in Oklahoma during the Depression's dust bowl years.
(Newbery Medal) Scholastic

A Single Shard
by Linda Sue Park
This is a tender tale of a twelfth-century Korean boy named Tree-ear who must overcome a host of obstacles in order to attain his life's dream. (Newbery Medal) Random House

Walk Two Moons
by Sharon Creech
After her mother leaves home suddenly, thirteen-year-old Sal and her eccentric grandparents take a car trip retracing her mother's route. Along the way, Sal entertains her grandparents with the story of her friend Phoebe. (Newbery Medal) HarperCollins

A Year Down Yonder
by Richard Peck
This Newbery-winning novel is set in 1937 in a tiny Illinois town. Told through the eyes of fifteen-year-old Mary Alice, this book is loaded with laughs as well as life lessons. Puffin

MYSTERY

Chasing Vermeer
by Blue Balliett
Petra and Calder work together to crack the mathematical trail left by an art thief in order to rescue a seventeenth-century Vermeer painting. Scholastic Press

I Dream of Murder
by Catherine Dexter
Jere doesn't know if his dream is a nightmare or a warning of the future. William Morrow

The Invention of Hugo Cabret
by Brian Selznick
Hugo, who makes his home in a Paris train station, learns that a mechanical man holds a secret from Hugo's dead father. Hugo must uncover the secret before it's too late.
Scholastic Press

Journey into Terror
by Bill Wallace
Before taking off for Oklahoma to see his father and his new family, Samuel Ross accidentally takes a picture that he shouldn't have. Now people are after him!
Simon & Schuster

Night of the Chupacabras
by Marie G. Lee
Lupe and her friends don't believe in bloodsucking creatures, but something is trying to change their minds. William Morrow

Orp and the FBI
by Suzy Kline
A mysterious intruder, a strange letter, and a vacant house combine to make an exciting mystery for twelve-year-old Orp. Penguin

Running Out of Time
by Margaret Peterson Haddix
When a diphtheria epidemic hits her 1840s village, thirteen-year-old Jessie discovers that her "village" is actually a 1996 tourist site under observation by heartless scientists. Simon & Schuster

Sebastian (Super Sleuth) and the Flying Elephant
by Mary Blount Christian
When Detective John Quincy Jones is told to find the circus's missing elephant by nightfall, his faithful canine companion must come to his rescue as usual. Macmillan

Stone Child
by Dan Poblocki
Eddie is thrilled when he moves to the hometown of his favorite author, Nathaniel Olmstead. His excitement turns to terror when the horrifying creatures of Olmstead's books begin appearing in his life. Yearling

The 39 Clues series
by a variety of authors
Orphans Amy and Dan Cahill risk death again and again to compete with other relatives for the family fortune, and solve a mystery, by collecting all 39 clues. Scholastic Press

Wait Till Helen Comes
by Mary Downing Hahn
Molly and Michael have never been fond of their stepsister, Heather. But when Heather begins warning them about a ghost named Helen, Molly begins to listen. Sandpiper

REALISTIC FICTION

Because of Winn-Dixie
by Kate DiCamillo
Because of Winn-Dixie, a big, unhappy, and ugly dog, ten-year-old Opal learns ten things about her long-gone mother from her preacher father. Opal begins to find her place in the world and let go of some of her sadness. (Newbery Honor) Candlewick Press

Bud, Not Buddy
by Christopher Paul Curtis
Times are tough in Flint, Michigan, in 1936, but ten-year-old Bud escapes a bad foster home and sets out in search of the man he believes is his true father—the famous band leader H. E. Calloway of Grand Rapids. (Newbery Medal) Random House

Carolina Crow Girl
by Valerie Hobbs
A crow brings a poor girl and a rich boy together. Farrar, Straus & Giroux

A Crooked Kind of Perfect
by Linda Urban
Zoe's father has overwhelming anxiety, her mother can't stop working, her classmate follows her home to spend time in the kitchen with her father, and Zoe ends up with a wheezy organ instead of the beautiful piano she dreams will take her to Carnegie Hall. Harcourt

Fourth Grade Rats
by Jerry Spinelli
Suds learns that his best friend is wrong: You don't have to be a tough guy, a "rat," to be a grown-up fourth grader. Scholastic

Frindle
by Andrew Clements
When fifth-grader Nick Allen invents a new word, he starts a chain of events that quickly gets beyond his control. Simon & Schuster

Hoot
by Carl Hiaasen
After moving to Florida, middle-schooler Roy Eberhardt teams up with the school bully and a runaway boy to protect underground owls from a proposed construction site. (Newbery Honor) Yearling

Joey Pigza Swallowed the Key
by Jack Gantos
Joey is faced with placement in special education classes unless he shapes up. HarperCollins

Just Juice
by Karen Hesse
It is up to nine-year-old Juice to help her father save their house by returning to school and learning how to read. Scholastic

Keep Ms. Sugarman in the Fourth Grade
by Elizabeth Levy
Jack's brief introduction to self-esteem by Ms. Sugarman is shattered when the teacher is promoted to principal in the middle of the year. HarperCollins

The Lemonade War
by Jacqueline Davies
Sibling rivalry heats up when Evan learns that his genius grade-skipping sister will be in his class this year. The two launch competing lemonade stands and battle for business and bragging rights. Houghton Mifflin Books for Children

A Llama in the Family
by Johanna Hurwitz
Sure that his birthday present will have two wheels and pedals, Adam is far from delighted when it turns out to have fur, four legs . . . and spits! William Morrow

Mockingbird
by Kathryn Erskine
Because of her Asperger's Syndrome, Caitlin sees the world in black and white, making it especially difficult for her to grieve after her brother is killed in a school shooting. Puffin

Navajo Summer
by Jennifer Owings Dewey
Jamie tries to escape her parents' divorce by running away to her Navajo friends. Sagebrush Education

Nerd No More
by Kristine L. Franklin
Wiggie is rejected after his mom stars in an educational science show. Candlewick Press

Sun & Spoon
by Kevin Hankes
After the death of his grandmother, ten-year-old Spoon tries to find the perfect keepsake to help him remember her. Puffin

Thank You, Mr. Falker
by Patricia Polacco
It is not until the fifth grade, when a new teacher arrives, that Tricia comes to understand and overcome her reading problem. Philomel

The View from Saturday
by E. L. Konigsburg
Four students, each with his or her own individual stories, develop a close bond and attract the attention of their teacher, a paraplegic, who chooses them to represent their sixth-grade class at the Academic Bowl competition. (Newbery Medal) Simon & Schuster

Wander
by Susan Hart Lindquist
Grieving for their dead mother, twelve-year-old James and his younger sister, Sary, find healing in their affection for a stray dog. Sagebrush Education

White Water
by P. J. Petersen
A young boy learns how to face his fears and find his courage on a white-water rafting trip with his adventure-loving father. Random House

Would My Fortune Cookie Lie?
by Stella Pevsner
Alexis doesn't know which is her bigger problem—moving or someone following her. Simon & Schuster

Zucchini Out West
by Barbara Dana
Billy learns that Zucchini might be an endangered ferret, so the creature can't be kept as a pet. HarperCollins

NONFICTION

BIOGRAPHY/AUTOBIOGRAPHY

The Abracadabra Kid: A Writer's Life
by Sid Fleischman
The Newbery-winning children's book writer recounts how he set out from childhood determined to be a magician. William Morrow

Anne Frank: The Diary of a Young Girl
by Anne Frank
This young girl shares her thoughts, fears, and dreams in her journal. A powerful account of a Jewish family during the Holocaust. Bantam

Basher Five-Two: The True Story of F-16 Fighter Pilot Captain Scott O'Grady
by Scott O'Grady
An F-16 fighter pilot tells his story. Bantam Doubleday Dell

Bull's-Eye: A Photobiography of Annie Oakley
by Sue Macy
National Geographic Society

Bully for You, Teddy Roosevelt
by Jean Fritz
This lively biography captures the exuberance and enthusiasm of president, conservationist, explorer, and author Theodore Roosevelt. Putnam

Childtimes: A Three-Generation Memoir
by Eloise Greenfield and Lessie Jones Little
In this lyrical memoir, three African-American women—a grandmother, daughter, and granddaughter—recreate their childhoods. HarperCollins

Christopher Reeve: Actor and Activist
by Margaret L. Finn
The life of the actor before and after his horseback riding accident. Chelsea House

Colin Powell: A Biography
by Jim Haskins
This biography traces the life of Colin Powell, the first African-American Chairman of the Joint Chiefs of Staff and the man who oversaw Operation Desert Storm. Scholastic

Confucius: The Golden Rule
by Russell Freedman
Newbery-winner Freedman delves deep into Chinese history in this intelligent and fun biography. Scholastic

The Double Life of Pocahontas
by Jean Fritz
A biography of the famous Native American princess, emphasizing her relationship with John Smith and the roles she played in two very different cultures. Putnam

Facing the Lion: Growing Up Maasai on the African Savanna
by Joseph Lemasolai Lekuton
This autobiography describes the author's extraordinary passage between cultures and his continuing effort to hold the two in balance. National Geographic Society

The First Woman Doctor
by Rachel Baker
This is an engrossing biography of Elizabeth Blackwell, the first female doctor, who also established a women's hospital and medical college. Scholastic

Four Perfect Pebbles: A Holocaust Story
by Lila Perl
Marion and her family try to escape the Holocaust. HarperCollins

Frederick Douglass Fights for Freedom
by Margaret Davidson
Born a slave, Frederick Douglass went on to become one of the most famous freedom fighters in modern times. Scholastic

How I Came to Be a Writer
by Phyllis Reynolds Naylor
In her autobiography, Newbery-winner Naylor details her career from grade school to the present. Simon & Schuster

Indian Chiefs
by Russell Freedman
Compelling profiles of six Native American chiefs who led their people through a historic crisis. The book includes photographs and a map. Holiday House

It Came from Ohio! My Life as a Writer
by R. L. Stine
R. L. Stine tells many of his "secrets" of how he became a writer and where he gets some of his ideas. Econo-Clad

Knots in My Yo-yo String: The Autobiography of a Kid
by Jerry Spinelli
The Newbery-winning children's author presents a humorous account of his childhood and youth in Norristown, Pennsylvania. Knopf

Knucklehead
by Jon Scieszka
Readers can explore the life and misadventures of author Jon Scieszka as he reminisces about military school, hand-me-down Halloween costumes, and rough-and-tumble fun with his five brothers. Viking Juvenile

Leon's Story
by Leon Walter Tillage
The son of a North Carolina sharecropper recalls the hard times his family and other African Americans faced in the first half of the twentieth century, and the changes the civil rights movement helped bring about. Farrar, Straus & Giroux

Looking Back: A Book of Memories
by Lois Lowry
Using family photographs and quotes from her books, the Newbery-winning author provides glimpses into her life. Houghton Mifflin

Lost Star: The Story of Amelia Earhart
by Patricia Lauber
A fascinating look at America's most famous female aviator. Scholastic

My Life in Dog Years
by Gary Paulsen
The author describes some of the dogs that have had special places in his life, including Dirk, who protected him from bullies, and Cookie, who saved his life. Bantam Doubleday Dell

Nelson Mandela: "No Easy Walk to Freedom"
by Barry Denenberg
The story of Mandela's remarkable life, from his boyhood to his twenty-six-year imprisonment to his release and visit to the United States. Scholastic

Of Beetles and Angels
by Mawi Asgedom
Though he delivered the 1999 commencement address at Harvard, Mawi Asgedom has not led a charmed life. He describes his family's flight from war-torn Ethiopia to a Sudanese refugee camp to Chicago, where the family must adjust to a foreign way of life.
Little, Brown Books for Young Readers

Pride of Puerto Rico: The Life of Roberto Clemente
by Paul Robert Walker
This biography traces the life of the baseball superstar who was noted for his achievements on and off the baseball field before his untimely death in an airplane crash. Harcourt

The Tarantula in My Purse: and 172 Other Wild Pets
by Jean Craighead George
A collection of autobiographical stories about the author's life, family, and many wild pets.
HarperCollins

Through My Eyes
by Ruby Bridges
Ruby remembers being the first child to integrate the New Orleans school system in 1960.
Scholastic

The Wall: Growing Up Behind the Iron Curtain
by Peter Sís
Using both artwork and journal entries to tell his tale, Caldecott artist Peter Sís recounts growing up in Czechoslovakia under Soviet rule. (Caldecott Honor) Farrar, Straus & Giroux

INFORMATIONAL BOOKS

Children of the Wild West
by Russell Freedman
Historical photographs and explanatory text present a picture of life in the American West from 1840 to the early 1900s. Houghton Mifflin

Elements
by Theodore Gray
This fascinating book contains photographic representations of the 118 elements in the periodic table. Black Dog & Leventhal Publishers

***Exploring the* Titanic**
by Robert D. Ballard
This book describes the luxury liner that sank in 1912 and the subsequent discovery and exploration of its underwater wreckage. Scholastic

Fields of Fury: The American Civil War
by James M. McPherson
Atheneum

Great Fire
by Jim Murphy
Told through the eyes of several survivors, this is a fascinating account of the infamous fire that destroyed most of Chicago in 1871. Scholastic

Hana's Suitcase
by Karen Levine
When a suitcase arrives at a children's Holocaust education center in Tokyo, Fumiko Ishioka tracks its path back to Hana Brady, a Czechoslovakian Jewish girl who died at Auschwitz. Albert Whitman & Company

How to Build Your Own Country
by Valerie Wyatt
illustrated by Fred Rix
This informative book does exactly what its title promises—it tells readers how to name a country, choose a motto, set up a government, and more. Kids Can Press, Limited

Immigrant Kids
by Russell Freedman
During the late 1800s and early 1900s, immigrant kids sold newspapers, hauled firewood, worked in sweatshops, and did many other kinds of labor. After work, they played, fought rivals, and became part of the fabric of American life. Puffin

In Defense of Liberty: The Story of America's Bill of Rights
by Russell Freedman
Discover the origins, applications, and challenges to the Bill of Rights, the ten amendments to the U.S. Constitution. Holiday House

Island of Hope: The Story of Ellis Island and the Journey to America
by Martin W. Sandler
Scholastic

Lincoln: A Photobiography
by Russell Freedman
The Newbery Medal book traces Lincoln's boyhood, marriage, young professional life, and presidency. Clarion

Math Dictionary
by Carol Vorderman
This comprehensive resource contains more than 300 entries to help students learn words, phrases, and concepts needed for math classes. DK Children

***Shipwreck at the Bottom of the World: The Extraordinary True Story of Shackelton and the* Endurance**
by Jennifer Armstrong
An exciting and fascinating account of the 1914 expedition that left Shackelton and his men shipwrecked on the frozen Antarctic Sea. Crown

Three Cups of Tea
by Greg Mortenson and David Oliver Relin
Because Pakistani villagers came to Greg Mortenson's aid following his attempt at the dangerous climb to the top of K2, the world's second tallest mountain, he promises to build them a school. He eventually helps build fifty-five schools in Taliban territory.
Penguin Books

The Top of the World: Climbing Mount Everest
by Steve Jenkins
Beautifully illustrated with cut-paper collage, this book delves into the story of the history, geography, climate, and dangers of the world's tallest mountain. Houghton Mifflin

Tornadoes
by Seymour Simon
The author describes the location, nature, development, and destructive effects of tornadoes, as well as how to stay out of danger. HarperCollins

Volcano: The Eruption and Healing of Mount St. Helens
by Patricia Lauber
An engaging account of how and why Mount St. Helens erupted in 1980 and the destruction it caused. The book also explores how life has returned to the area. Simon & Schuster

We Are the Ship
by Kadir Nelson
The players of Negro League baseball overcame racial discrimination and persecution to pursue this truly American pastime. Hyperion/Jump at the Sun

Weather
by Seymour Simon
The author describes the causes of weather and its changing patterns. There is also a section on forecasting weather. HarperCollins

Who Really Discovered America? Unraveling the Mystery and Solving the Puzzle
by Avery Hart
This book not only questions theories about America's discovery but also encourages readers to keep an open mind and think for themselves. Ideals Publication

Working With Wildlife: A Guide to Careers in the Animal World
by Thane Maynard
Many students dream of working with wildlife, but don't know how to go about making their dreams come true. This informational guide provides answers, focusing on both common and uncommon careers with animals. Scholastic

The Wright Brothers: How They Invented the Airplane
by Russell Freedman
This book explores the lives and achievements of Orville and Wilbur Wright. Their achievements are documented in photographs as well as words. Holiday House

Index

M

N

O

P

W